COLORADO
SCENIC GUIDE
SOUTHERN REGION

COLORADO
SCENIC GUIDE
SOUTHERN REGION

Lee Gregory

Johnson Books: Boulder

Cover photo: Great Sand Dunes National Monument by Robert Schram

Cover design by Robert Schram

Second Edition
1   2   3   4   5   6   7   8   9

ISBN 1-55566-063-0
LCCCN 84-80536

Printed in the United States of America by
Johnson Publishing Company
1880 South 57th Court
Boulder, Colorado 80301

ACKNOWLEDGEMENTS

A project of this size requires help from many people. I would like to thank all who have assisted in this undertaking, even if I was not fortunate enough to know all their names so that they could be listed here.

Many friends have spent long hours reading through my manuscript to correct spelling and grammatical errors. For this effort, I thank Sonje and Ken Jessen, Steve Reames, Bonnie and Bill Spaulding, and Katie and Charlie Potter. I would also like to thank friends who contributed photos and research material, provided transportation, and offered encouragement, including Steve Reames, Ken Jessen, Lynn Schmidt, Bob Sobol, Joe Marriott, and Mary Lee and Walt Gregory.

Many government agencies and private individuals have provided information, photographs, and checks for accuracy. Gratitude is owed to the helpful employees of the National Park Service, the United States Department of Agriculture Forest Service, the Bureau of Land Management, the United States Geological Survey, and the state of Colorado. In particular, I would like to thank Jack Rathbone; Mel Griffiths; Andrew J. Kordziel, Angelina Valverde, Andrew J. Senti, Cindy McKee, Jon Wesley Sering, Wade Johnson, and Evaline Olson (BLM); the staffs of Pike, San Isabel, Grand Mesa, Uncompahgre, Gunnison, Rio Grande, and San Juan National Forests; Raymond J. Evans, Joseph J. Newton, Arnie Arneson, Karl L. Tameler, James R. Hillis, Thomas E. Lonberger, Dennis Neill, and Andre J. Coisman (USFS); Dwight F. Canfield, Carol Edwards, and Hal Chantker (USGS); Harris R. Feathers (USDA); Michael L. Baugher (USDI); the staffs of Colorado National Monument, Hovenweep National Monument, Mesa Verde National Park, Black Canyon of the Gunnison National Monument, Great Sand Dunes National Monument, Curecanti National Recreation Area, and Bent's Fort National Historic Site; Jack L. Muller, Duncan R. Burchard, Nancy Jane Cushing, John H. Trimble, Dennis K. Huffman, Hank Schoch, Robert C. Reyes, and Robert L. Schultz (NPS); NASA; Cheryl Brchan (Colorado Geological Survey); Gregg Chancellor and Hal Haney (Colorado Office of Tourism); Virginia and Alton Cole (Creede); George Chapman and Allen Nossaman (Silverton); and David R. Koch (Ouray).

I would also like to thank the people at Colorado Color who converted my color slides to black and white prints and Barbara Mussil, Michael McNierney, David Morgan, Terri Carr, Mark Vollmar, Ron Blommel and all the people of Johnson Publishing Company who helped put this book together. Particular thanks go to the late Malcolm Harris and his family who went out of their way to help out.

San Juan Mountains, southwestern Colorado.

This work is dedicated to Katie, Charlie, Bill, Julie, Bruce, and Steve, who helped me survive the two best desert backpacking trips of my life.

TABLE OF CONTENTS

TABLE OF CONTENTS

SCENERY COVERED BY THIS GUIDE

Colorado has something for everyone. If you're interested in scenery, archaeology, mining history, paleontology, hiking, old railroads, backpacking, Indian history, mountain climbing, or exploring, this is the place to visit. This guide is designed to help sightseers, both residents and tourists, get the most from their Colorado travels.

Colorado is so diversified that a guidebook such as this is difficult to produce; the research and exploration are fun, but it's painful having to decide what material to leave out. In the six years of research that have gone into this book, I have read volumes of background material, studied layers of maps, evaluated piles of photographs, and visited over 1000 scenic locations. From this, I have selected 100 sites that I think best represent the quality and diversity of Colorado's scenery. Fifty of these are included in this guide. The remaining 50 sites have been published in a companion volume covering the northern region of the state.

The sites included here are representative of the best scenery southern Colorado has to offer. Apart from locations of exceptional historic and scenic value, few man-made sites are included. All of the national parks and monuments open to the public within the southern region of the state are included.

This guide is primarily intended for the motorist. Of the 50 sites, 43 can be reached by passenger car. Two additional sites have rough access roads that are passable by two-wheel-drive vehicles with good ground clearance. Four sites are best visited by four-wheel-drive vehicles, but each has a worthwhile portion of scenery that can be enjoyed by passenger car. Only one site requires lengthy hiking.

I hope this book can convey at least a small portion of the enjoyment and fascination I have experienced while hiking, driving, four-wheeling, and flying through Colorado. I consider it a privilege to share this wonderful place with you. I hope you'll find this guide entertaining as well as useful. Enjoy Colorado's magnificent scenery!

SCENERY COVERED BY THIS GUIDE

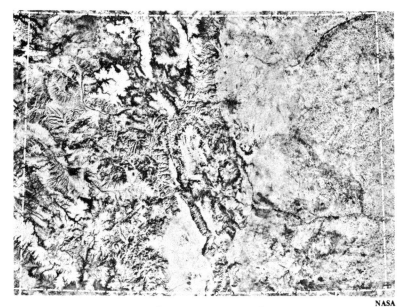

Satellite photo of Colorado.

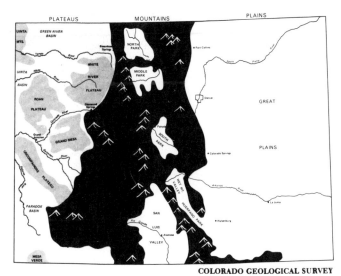

The three major geologic zones of Colorado.

PRECAUTIONS

Although visiting and enjoying Colorado scenery is not generally hazardous, the following list of suggestions may be useful in planning for maximum comfort, safety, and convenience. This section identifies potential hazards so they won't come as a complete surprise and points out that there are dangers to the environment as well. Common sense is almost always the best course. There are several excellent books available that cover wilderness safety and etiquette in greater detail than is offered here.

- Don't drink untreated water.

- Climb to higher ground if rising water indicates the danger of a flash flood.

- Return to lower elevations if symptoms of altitude sickness appear (nausea or shortness of breath).

- Wear sunglasses and protective skin creams to guard against the sun's ultraviolet rays. (This is especially important if you are around snow on sunny days.)

- Leave animals alone.

- Retreat if road conditions are too rough or hazardous for your vehicle.

- Plan to return from the backcountry before dark.

- Never trespass.

- If you are exposed to a lightning hazard (indicated by a crackle of static electricity, ionizing or glowing air, or your hair standing on end), retreat to the lowest area that you can reach quickly and crouch into a low position with your feet held tightly together as your only contact with the ground.

- Be aware that distances given on signs are not always accurate.

- Stay on established roads.

- Lock your car.

- Be careful with fire while camping.

- Pack out your trash when you leave the backcountry.

- Don't throw rocks over the edge.

PRECAUTIONS

In your vehicle you should carry:

- Food and water

- Warm clothing

- Sleeping bags or blankets (during winter)

- Chains (useful in both mud and snow)

- Tools and spare parts

- A reliable spare tire

- A flashlight

- A first-aid kit

- A compass

While hiking:

- Be prepared for any kind of weather.

- Retreat if storms approach.

- Take cover in a bad hail storm.

- Be careful where you place hands and feet while in areas that may contain rattlesnakes (plateaus, plains, and valleys below 8,000 feet).

- Check for ticks (sometimes abundant in moist, vegetated areas) during the wet part of spring (usually May and early June).

- Stay on established trails.

- For longer hikes, carry a flashlight, food, and water.

KEY TO INFORMATION BLOCK

TYPE: This entry identifies the scenic nature of the site.

ADMINISTRATION: This entry identifies ownership of the site. Land administration is subject to change. Even if this guidebook indicates the site was once on public land, please do not trespass if that land is now marked as private. In the case of private property, please view the site from public land or a public road. Never enter private land without the specific permission of the landowner. National parks, monuments, recreation areas, forests, and grasslands as well as Bureau of Land Management areas and sites administered by state, county, and local governments are open to the public, though a visitation fee may apply.

QUALITY: The relative scenic quality of each site is described by the following terms in order of least scenic to most scenic: SCENIC, VERY SCENIC, EXTREMELY SCENIC, SUPERBLY SCENIC.

ACCESS: This category describes the most difficult type of road encountered on the way to the site. Road conditions are subject to change. Regardless of what this guidebook indicates, if the road appears to be more difficult than for what you and your vehicle are equipped, do not attempt it. Sometimes the difficult part is near the end of the route. You can often get within walking distance before the road becomes too rough. In the case of four-wheel-drive (4WD) roads, there is usually some scenic aspect that can be enjoyed by travelers not having a four-wheel-drive vehicle. In these cases, the extent of what can be seen by passenger car is usually discussed in the description of the site. The following list gives the possible entries for the ACCESS category and their meanings:

PAVED ROAD: These sites are accessible by any passenger car.

GOOD DIRT ROAD: This kind of road is generally passable in either wet or dry weather.

DIRT ROAD: This type of road is usually passable under dry conditions but can become very muddy and potentially impassable when thoroughly wet.

ROUGH DIRT ROAD: This type of road may contain potholes, bumps, ruts, rocks, stream crossings, and slight sideways tilts. It may be impassable when wet. Passenger cars that travel this kind of road need a careful driver and at least average ground clearance. Two-wheel-drive vehicles with good ground clearance, such as pick-up trucks, should have no trouble.

EASY 4WD: Access to these sites requires a four-wheel-drive vehicle. Roads of this type are too rough or steep for passenger cars. A two-wheel-drive vehicle with good ground clearance, such as a pick-up truck, can sometimes negotiate these roads.

MODERATE 4WD: A four-wheel-drive vehicle is required to visit these sites. The driver may have to work a little to traverse this type of road.

DIFFICULT 4WD: These roads are not for beginners. A certain amount of four-wheel-drive experience and skill may be required to safely negotiate the road.

HIKE: A walk of over a half-mile is required to reach the site.

FACILITIES: Visitor facilities are listed under this heading.

TIME NEEDED: Indicated is the minimum time needed to visit the site. In general, this does not include access time needed to reach the scenic location. However, it will include some of the driving time if the access is part of enjoying the scenery of the specific site.

BEST VISIT: This entry gives the best, but not the only, time of year to visit the site. Here, "best" is a combination of ease of access, personal comfort, and optimal scenic quality. In years of heavy snowfall, some sites may be blocked until much later than is indicated. Light snow years may offer earlier access. Many sites are particularly beautiful during the last weeks of September and the first weeks of October when the aspens turn color. The entries in this category are generally self-explanatory, but there is sometimes implied information in their recommendations, as indicated below:

SPRING OR FALL: These sites may be uncomfortably hot in summer.

MIDSUMMER TO LATE SUMMER: This entry refers to sites whose access is often blocked by snow well into summer. These same locations are sometimes cut off by early snows in September. Mid-July is not an unusual date for the higher sites to become accessible.

EARLY SUMMER TO FALL: Snow often blocks these sites during winter.

JULY: Waterfalls are usually most spectacular during this month.

BEST PHOTO: This category recommends the best, but not the only, time of day to photograph the site. In this case, "best" is when the natural lighting is optimal to photograph some distinctive aspect of the scenery. This assumes, of course, that the weather is cooperating—which it often doesn't. It is typical for mountain skies to become cloudy during the late afternoon in Colorado, even on days that start out clear. This entry may cover a wide portion of the day if numerous photographic opportunities

KEY TO INFORMATION BLOCK

exist. Possible entries are listed below with typical times pertaining to a long, midsummer's day:

EARLY MORNING: Sunrise to 9:00 AM.

MORNING: 8:00 AM to 11:00 AM.

MIDDAY: 10:00 AM to 2:00 PM.

AFTERNOON: 1:00 PM to 5:00 PM.

LATE AFTERNOON: 4:00 PM to sunset.

ELEVATION: This category gives the altitude of the site in feet above sea level.

REFERENCE: This category gives an easy-to-find location used in the directions. The reference can be a city, an intersection of two well-identified highways, a well-marked mountain pass, or sometimes the intersection of a highway with a state or county line. An attempt has been made to select reference locations that are not likely to change with time. Reference locations can be found on the state highway map issued by the state of Colorado as well as on most other varieties of Colorado state highway maps.

MAP: This category lists the most convenient maps for locating the site. This is generally the state highway map, a United States Forest Service visitor map, a United States Geological Survey topographical map, or a Bureau of Land Management (BLM) map. The state highway map is listed if it shows all roads necessary to get to the site, even if the site itself is not identified.

USGS TOPO: This category gives the United States Geological Survey topographical maps of the 7.5 or 15 minute series that include the site. Maps of the 7.5 minute series offer high resolution with a scale of 1:24,000, and maps of the 15 minute series offer a scale of 1:62,500. All of the maps listed in this category are from the Colorado index of available USGS maps. This entry contains the name of the map, either 7.5′ or 15′ notation to identify the series, and the date of release or latest revision.

USGS COUNTY: This lists the United States Geological Survey county series topographic maps that cover the site. This series offers good resolution at 1:50,000 scale.

KEY TO INFORMATION BLOCK

DIRECTIONS: The directions section contains accurate instructions on how to find the site. The directions give a route that begins with, or includes, the reference location that is listed in the information block. All of the directions were gathered during visits to the individual sites and were rechecked in 1982. For the second edition, almost all sites were revisited in 1989.

Unfortunately, directions are sometimes subject to change. If you are trying to locate a site and find that road intersections, turns, and landmarks are not where the instructions indicate, you will have to do your own navigation to reach that location. The maps supplied should prove handy in this case. If the access has been denied because it crosses private land, please do not attempt to approach the site by trespassing.

Cumulative mileages in the directions (enclosed by brackets: "< >") are given with respect to a beginning reference location. In general, distances are measured from the middle of locations. This applies to small towns, landmarks, tunnels, and the like. When this is not the case, the directions will indicate that the mileage refers to the beginning, end, entrance, or exit of some point of reference. For road intersections, distances are measured from the center of the intersection. Distances from highway interchanges (overpass or underpass) are measured from the middle of the roads where they cross each other.

The distances in the directions were measured by precalibrated odometer readings during visits to the sites. You may wish to calibrate your own odometer against mile-markers found on all Colorado interstate highways. Mileages that contain a decimal point and a tenths digit are intended to be accurate to the nearest tenth of a mile. Some sites are so well marked and so hard to miss that more casual directions are given.

MAPS

Each item contains one or more maps for use with the directions to locate the site. These maps may also be handy for exploring some of the surrounding area not specifically discussed in the text. The source maps used sometimes show roads that are no longer accessible or passable. Even though an indicated road may still exist, its condition may have changed, making access either less or more difficult than the map shows. New roads may not be shown at all. Property ownership may have changed, resulting in reduced access. All of this depends on when the base maps used in this guide were last updated by the originating agency. The possibility of these variations should be taken into account.

The maps listed for each site cover only a small area and are intended to be used with the district map which is provided at the beginning of each district grouping of scenic sites. These district maps show the location of all the nearby sites included in a sizable portion of the state. A state map showing the location of all items in this book appears at the end of this chapter. A companion state highway map may be useful for navigation while on the road, and topographic maps with a high degree of resolution should be used as navigation aids to sites that require extensive hiking.

Maps included in this guide are excerpts from larger maps produced by state or federal government agencies. A scale indicator is given on each map. True north is always toward the top of the page unless otherwise indicated. The courtesy line at the bottom of each map identifies the originating government agency and implies which map key should be used to identify the meaning of the black and white symbols used on that map. These map keys follow this section and are arranged according to the originating map agency. No key is needed for maps generated by the National Park Service (NPS) and other agencies that use self-explanatory symbols.

MAP OVERPRINT KEY

All maps used in this guide are overprinted with information in red to aid in finding the route to the site. The overprint symbols are:

■ Reference location used in directions

➤ ➤ ➤ Vehicular route

▲ Vista, overlook, or point of interest

------ Foot trail

★ Scenic item

⊢ 1 M ⊣ Scale of miles

USDA FOREST SERVICE MAP KEY

LEGEND

———————	National Forest Boundary	🏕	Recreation Site
—— ——	Adjacent National Forest Boundary		Recreation Site other than Forest Service
—— - ——	County Boundary Line		Ski Area
—— · —— · ——	Reservation Boundary	▲	Observation Site
▦▦▦▦▦▦	Wilderness or Special Area Boundary	◆	Point of Interest
(70)	Interstate Highway	●	Visitors Center
(285)	U.S. Highway	.	House, Cabin or other Building
(9)	State Highway	——	Dam
[112]	Forest Route	○	Well
———————	Paved Road		Water Well
———————	All Weather Road	—+—-—+—	Railroad Tunnel
———————	Dirt Road		National Park or Monument
===⊐===⁴ᵂᴰ—	Primitive Road and Four Wheel Drive		(Land ownership within boundary not shown) National Recreation Area
███□███²¹⁵	Freeway with Interchange		State Land (Permission required to enter)
— — — — —	Trail		Arapaho National Forest Land
🛆	District Ranger Station		Adjacent National Forest Land
🛆	Forest Service Station		BLM Land
✕	Mine, Quarry or Gravel Pit		

Supervisors Headquarters, Fort Collins, Colorado

TOWNSHIP AND SECTION LINE CLASSIFICATION

——— Surveyed, location reliable

—— —— Surveyed, location approximate

— — — — Unsurveyed (Bureau of Land Management protraction)

Courtesy of USDA Forest Service

BUREAU OF LAND MANAGEMENT MAP KEY

MAP SYMBOLS

Feature	Symbol	Feature	Symbol	Feature	Symbol	Feature	Symbol	Feature	Symbol
District Bdy	▬▬▬	Road All Weather	Divided	Principal Access	Divided	Buildings	▪	Towns and Cities	
Nat'l or State	▬ ▬ ▬	Road Seasonal Use	- - - - -			Buildings (Abandoned)	▫	River or Large Stream	
		Road "Jeep" Type "Primitive"	- ▪ - ▪ -	Road Interchange	⊃○	BLM Office	▲	Stream	
Continental Divide	▬ ▬	Trail	- - - - -	Rest Area	⊃	School	▪	Large Dam	
County	▬ ▬ ▬	Railroad Double Track	+—+—+			Church	▲	Reservoir or Retention Dam	
Land Grant	▬ ▪▪	Railroad Single Track	+—+			Radio Installation	▲	Lake or Pond	
Miscellaneous (Res., etc.)	▬ ▪ ▬	Glacier		Levee or Dike		Fire Lookout (Primary)	▲	Intermittent Lake or Pond	
Park (State, County or Local)	▬ ▬ ▬	Road Bridge		Corral	⌒	Fire Lookout (Secondary)	⊚	Dry Lake or Pond	
Township and Range	Surveyed ___ Protracted _ _	Railroad Bridge		Recreation Site	△	Fire Tool Cache	▪	Marsh	
Section	Surveyed ___ Protracted _ _	Foot Bridge		Tanks-(label as to type)	⊙	Shelter	▫	Spring	O→
Sec., Status Subdivision	....	Ferry	) ▪ (	Oil or Gas Wells	○	Cliff Dwelling	▫	Improved Spring	O→
Section Identification	6	Road Ford	=‡=	Mine or Quarry	✕	Ruins Small / Large	▫ Ruins / Ruins	Well	○
State Plane Coordinates And Zone	1,500,000 E	Trail Ford	-‡-	US Mineral or Location Monument	▲	Cemetery	CEM	Artesian Well	⊚
Boundary Monument	-⊙-	Road Tunnel	⊐ - ⊏	Located Object (Labeled)	⊙	Sawmill	▲	Windmill	△
Route Marker Interstate	⬤	Railroad Tunnel	⊐ - ⊏	Triangulation Station	△ Dog	Airfield	⊢	Aqueduct Tunnel	→▬←←
Route Marker U.S.	⬠			Bluffs or Cliffs				Ditch or Canal	→—←
Route Marker State	◯	Prominent Peak	⬧	Prominent Ridge		Gaging Station	✦	Aqueduct	→—→→

UNITED STATES GEOLOGIC SURVEY MAP KEY

Primary highway, hard surface . . . .

Secondary highway, hard surface . . . .

Light-duty road, hard or improved surface . . . .

Unimproved road . . . .

Road under construction, alinement known . . . .

Proposed road . . . .

Dual highway, dividing strip 25 feet or less . . . .

Dual highway, dividing strip exceeding 25 feet . . . .

Trail . . . .

Railroad: single track and multiple track . . . .

Railroads in juxtaposition . . . .

Narrow gage: single track and multiple track . . . .

Railroad in street and carline . . . .

Bridge: road and railroad . . . .

Drawbridge: road and railroad . . . .

Footbridge . . . .

Tunnel: road and railroad . . . .

Overpass and underpass . . . .

Small masonry or concrete dam . . . .

Dam with lock . . . .

Dam with road . . . .

Canal with lock . . . .

Buildings (dwelling, place of employment, etc.) . . . .

School, church, and cemetery . . . .

Buildings (barn, warehouse, etc.) . . . .

Power transmission line with located metal tower . . . .

Telephone line, pipeline, etc. (labeled as to type) . . . .

Wells other than water (labeled as to type) . . . . ○ Oil . . . . . ○ Gas

Tanks: oil, water, etc. (labeled only if water) . . . . ● ● ● ⊘ Water

Located or landmark object; windmill . . . . ○ . . . . ⌁

Open pit, mine, or quarry; prospect . . . . ⤬ . . . . ×

Shaft and tunnel entrance . . . . ■ . . . . Y

Horizontal and vertical control station:

    Tablet, spirit level elevation . . . . BM △ 5653

    Other recoverable mark, spirit level elevation . . . . △ 5455

Horizontal control station: tablet, vertical angle elevation VABM △ 95/9

    Any recoverable mark, vertical angle or checked elevation △ 3775

Vertical control station: tablet, spirit level elevation . . . . . BM × 957

    Other recoverable mark, spirit level elevation . . . . × 954

Spot elevation . . . . × 7369 × 7369

Water elevation 670

Courtesy of USGS

UNITED STATES GEOLOGIC SURVEY MAP KEY

Boundaries: National . . . .

    State . . . .

    County, parish, municipio . . . .

    Civil township, precinct, town, barrio . . . .

    Incorporated city, village, town, hamlet . . . .

    Reservation, National or State . . . .

    Small park, cemetery, airport, etc. . . . .

    Land grant . . . .

Township or range line, United States land survey . . . . . .

Township or range line, approximate location . . . .

Section line, United States land survey . . . .

Section line, approximate location . . . .

Township line, not United States land survey . . . .

Section line, not United States land survey . . . .

Found corner: section and closing . . . .

Boundary monument: land grant and other . . . .

Fence or field line . . . .

Index contour . . . .   Intermediate contour . .

Supplementary contour   Depression contours . .

Fill . . . .   Cut . . . .

Levee . . . .   Levee with road . . . . .

Mine dump . . . .   Wash . . . .

Tailings . . . .   Tailings pond . . . .

Shifting sand or dunes   Intricate surface . . . . .

Sand area . . . .   Gravel beach . . . .

Perennial streams . . . .   Intermittent streams . .

Elevated aqueduct . . . .   Aqueduct tunnel . . . . .

Water well and spring .   Glacier . . . .

Small rapids . . . .   Small falls . . . .

Large rapids . . . .   Large falls . . . .

Intermittent lake . . . . .   Dry lake bed . . . .

Foreshore flat . . . .   Rock or coral reef . . . .

Sounding, depth curve .   Piling or dolphin . . . . .

Exposed wreck . . . .   Sunken wreck . . . .

Rock, bare or awash; dangerous to navigation . . . .

Marsh (swamp) . . . . . .   Submerged marsh . . .

Wooded marsh . . . .   Mangrove . . . .

Woods or brushwood . .   Orchard . . . .

Vineyard . . . .   Scrub . . . .

Land subject to
controlled inundation   Urban area . . . .

Courtesy of USGS

STATE MAP

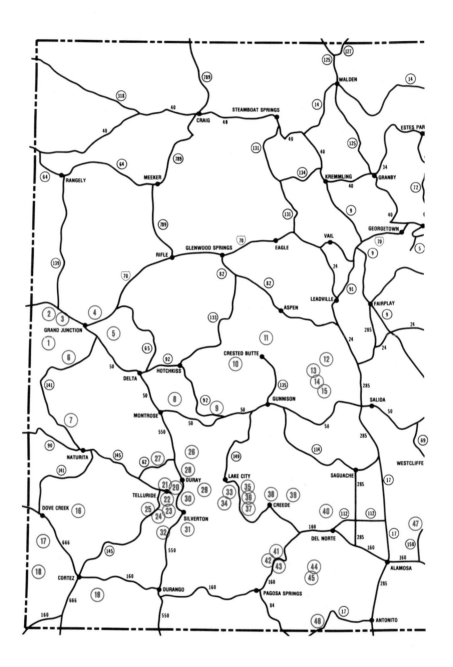

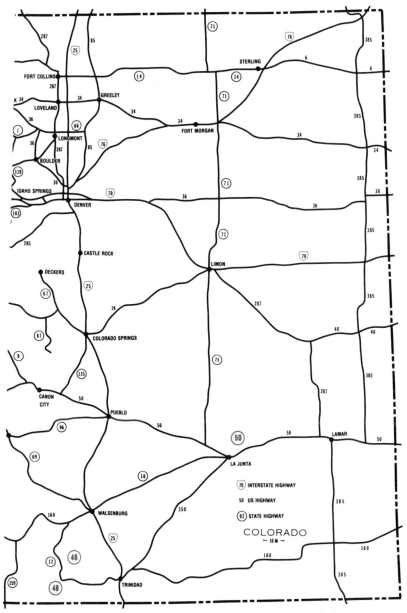

Cartography by Lee Gregory

GRAND JUNCTION DISTRICT

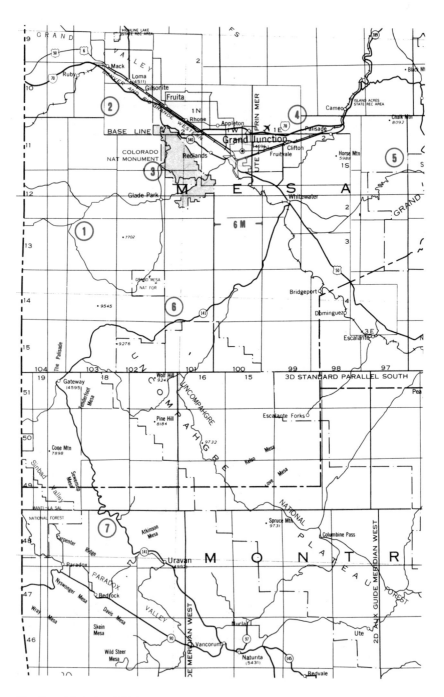

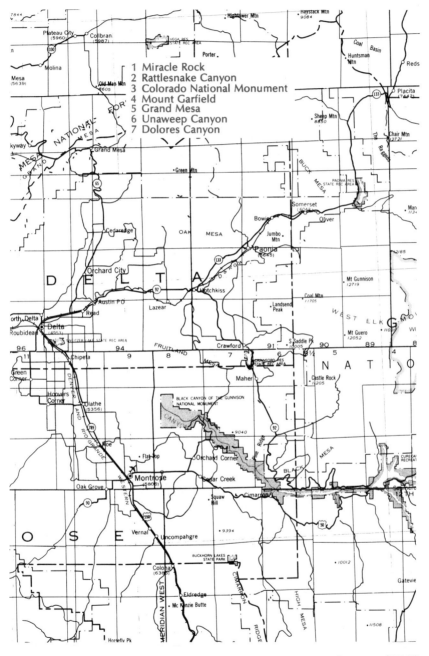

1 Miracle Rock
2 Rattlesnake Canyon
3 Colorado National Monument
4 Mount Garfield
5 Grand Mesa
6 Unaweep Canyon
7 Dolores Canyon

Courtesy of USGS

1 MIRACLE ROCK

TYPE: Plateau Scenery/Geologic
ADMINISTRATION: BLM land
QUALITY: Scenic
ACCESS: Good dirt road
FACILITIES: Picnic area/Rest rooms/Nearby campground
TIME NEEDED: Half hour
BEST VISIT: Spring or fall
BEST PHOTO: Morning or afternoon
ELEVATION: 6,790 feet
REFERENCE: Glade Park
MAP: BLM Delta 1:100,000
USGS TOPO: Payne Wash 7.5' (1972)
USGS COUNTY: Mesa County Sheet 1 of 6 (1975)

Miracle Rock is a huge sandstone boulder precariously balanced on the rim of a sheer cliff. The rock stands thirty feet tall, weighs an estimated 12,000 tons, and is balanced on a pedestal that may be as small as three square feet. Some sources claim it to be the largest balanced rock in the world. A claim such as this is hard to prove, but record holder or not, it is certainly an awesome sight. Erosion created this phenomenon and will eventually destroy it. Some day perhaps, Miracle Rock will creak, teeter, and then tumble to the floor of the valley, some 200 feet below.

DIRECTIONS: Inside Colorado National Monument (see site 3 for directions), there is a junction of the paved Glade Park Road and Rim Rock Drive, the main road through Colorado National Monument, 3.8 miles from the east entrance station and 18.5 miles from the west entrance station. This junction <0.0> is marked by a brown sign identifying a turn for Glade Park, Glade Park Store (5 miles), and Piñon Mesa. Turn here and head south, then west, toward Glade Park on the paved road, leaving Colorado National Monument <0.7>.

At the crossroads <5.8> at the Glade Park Store, a sign on the left side of the road displays a map showing Miracle Rock and nearby campgrounds. Continue straight at this intersection and you will eventually descend into a pleasant, wide, flat valley. The pavement ends <8.6>, and you continue on a good dirt road. Turn left onto a dirt road <13.8> (9.8 Road). Continue to a sign <14.9> that marks Miracle Rock Recreation Site. Turn left and follow the short loop road to the parking area <15.0>. To find Miracle Rock, walk through the picnic tables to a sign reading: "Miracle Rock Trail, 500 yards." Follow this trail uphill to the balanced rock.

The loop road takes you back to the dirt road, where you may wish to turn left and continue 1.3 miles to the Falls Campground. To reach the Little Dolores Falls, enter the campground, follow the loop road to the back and right of the campground, stop, and walk away from the main campground to reach the falls, just outside the campground boundary.

Huge Miracle Rock is precariously balanced at the edge of a cliff.

1 MIRACLE ROCK

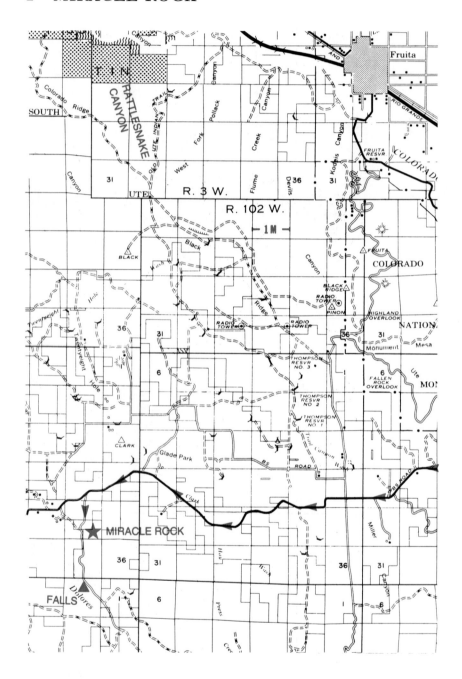

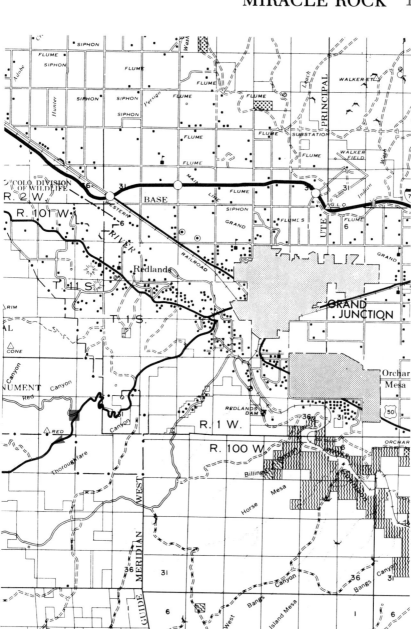

Courtesy of BLM

2 RATTLESNAKE CANYON

TYPE:	Plateau Scenery/Geologic
ADMINISTRATION:	BLM land
QUALITY:	Extremely scenic
ACCESS:	Rough dirt road and hike
FACILITIES:	None
TIME NEEDED:	Four hours
BEST VISIT:	Spring or fall
BEST PHOTO:	Midday to afternoon
ELEVATION:	5,600 feet (rim containing arches)
REFERENCE:	Fruita
MAP:	BLM Grand Junction 1:100,000
USGS TOPO:	Mack 7.5′ (1973)
USGS COUNTY:	Mesa County Sheet 1 of 6 (1975)

Rattlesnake Canyon contains a large concentration of natural rock arches, similar to Arches National Park, 100 miles to the west. The arches, in various stages of formation, have been carved by erosion in a rim of Entrada sandstone atop the red and tan banded walls of the canyon. There are at least a dozen arches in the upper portions of the canyon. The largest of these resembles a flying buttress about 120 feet high and 80 feet across. The smallest is an arch in the making, a small hole that has recently opened in the roof of a rock dome. It is best to stay off this thin rock.

This canyon receives little visitation because it is remote, undeveloped, and hard to reach. The dirt road leading to the canyon, at best, is rough. It should be attempted only by vehicles with high ground clearance; four-wheel-drive helps. When the road is wet, however, it is impassable even with four-wheel-drive. The trip in takes at least an hour under ideal conditions. Once at the canyon, you can encircle about nine arches with a two-mile walk. Also, look across the canyon for an arch on the west rim. Rattlesnakes are no more of a hazard here than elsewhere in canyon country, but beware of the summer heat and the vicious gnats that infest the area in late May and early June. Carry water.

DIRECTIONS: Inside Colorado National Monument (see site 3 for directions), 11.5 miles from the east entrance station and 10.8 miles from the west entrance station, there is a junction of Rim Rock Drive (the main road through Colorado National Monument) and a gravel road to the Glade Park Store. This junction <0.0> is marked by a small sign identifying a turn for the Glade Park Store (5 miles). Follow this gravel road outside the monument <0.1> to a dirt road <0.2> on the right, marked by a sign saying: "Black Ridge Road."

Beyond here, it is easy to get lost; follow the mileages carefully. Turn right onto this rough dirt road. Continue to a T-intersection <1.5> and turn right; you will see an airplane beacon ahead. Continue and then turn left

LEE GREGORY

To reach the lower level, climb down through this magnificent arch.

LEE GREGORY

Numerous arches can be found along the eastern rim of the canyon.

onto the main dirt road <1.9> at the brow of a hill. At this intersection, ignore the road that continues straight toward the beacon and a lesser road that goes to the left up a hill. Ignore a side road <2.2> on the right and a side road <5.4> on the left. Continue past a side road <5.5> on the right. Bear right where a steep, descending road <8.7> joins from the left. You are now headed toward the Colorado River (very rough road). Bear right where a road <9.4> joins from the left (access to the west rim of Rattlesnake Canyon). You are now parallel to the east rim of Rattlesnake Canyon; an arch is visible <10.4> on the canyon's west rim.

Vehicles must stop at the small turnaround at the top of a steep hill <11.0>. You must walk the next mile. Follow the Upper Arches Trail (old road). Just past a narrow neck, the road approaches the white sandstone of the rim. Search up-canyon (south) for the most southerly arch. You then walk down to the next lower level through the huge arch. (This descent is intimidating; you may wish to use the longer Lower Arches Trail whose sign you passed on the old road.) Once you have reached the lower level, circle to your right and walk down-canyon (north) along this level ledge, observing the arches above you in the rim. After three-quarters of a mile, you reach the mouth of the canyon. Circle to the right around the point and scramble up a slope in the wall to the top of the rim, return the way you came, or return on the Lower Arches Trail.

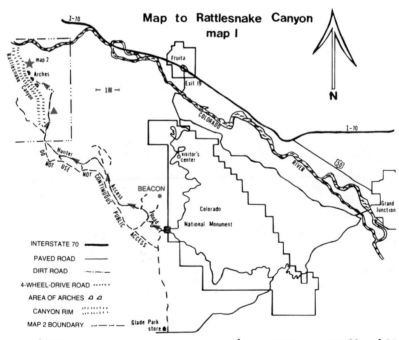

Courtesy of BLM

Also see map on pages 30 and 31.

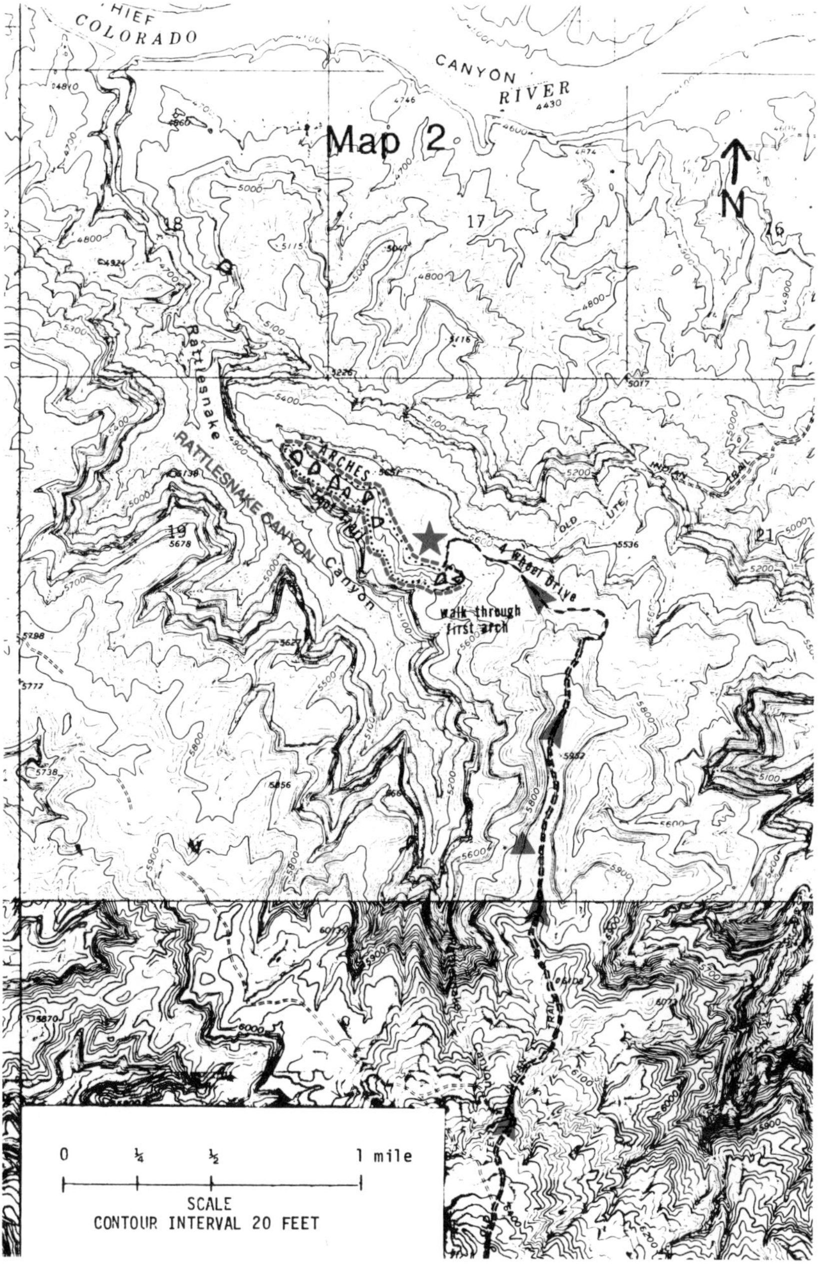

Map 2

Courtesy of BLM

3 COLORADO NATIONAL MONUMENT

TYPE: Plateau Scenery/Geologic
ADMINISTRATION: National Monument
QUALITY: Very scenic
ACCESS: Paved road
FACILITIES: Visitor center/Campground/Picnic areas
TIME NEEDED: Half day
BEST VISIT: Spring or fall
BEST PHOTO: Afternoon to late afternoon
ELEVATION: 5,787 feet (visitor center)
REFERENCE: Fruita
MAP: State highway map
USGS TOPO: Colorado National Monument 7.5' (1973)
USGS COUNTY: Mesa County Sheet 1 of 6 (1975)

Colorado National Monument encompasses a series of sheer-walled sandstone canyons at the southern edge of Grand Valley. The same layers of sandstone that form these canyon walls are still buried beneath the floor of this valley. Colorado National Monument marks the northern rim of the Uncompahgre Plateau, a region that has undergone a series of recurrent uplifts over a period of millions of years. Water draining into Grand Valley from the plateau has carved these colorful canyons, exposing a thick sequence of sedimentary rocks. Wingate sandstone forms the vertical walls, and the canyon rims are Kayenta sandstone.

Long before the Uncompahgre Plateau was uplifted, dinosaurs roamed the area, and portions of several large skeletons have been found nearby. Some of the early human inhabitants of the area were the Fremont Indians, contemporaries of the Anasazi. The Fremont Culture left a legacy of petroglyphs, or rock art, on smooth sandstone at several sites within the monument. Artifacts and living sites of this culture have also been discovered. About A.D. 1200, the ancestors of the present Ute Indians moved into the area. The 1776 Dominguez-Escalante Expedition passed the monument on their way north. The purpose of this Spanish journey was to find a route linking Santa Fe, New Mexico, with the California missions. In 1830 a trading post was established a distance to the south by Antoine Robidoux to serve the independent fur trappers and mountain men of the region. John W. Gunnison passed the monument in 1853 while conducting a survey for a transcontinental railroad route. After the Utes were forced from western Colorado in the 1880s, settlers began to populate Grand Valley.

The most important person in the monument's history is undoubtedly John Otto. He arrived in 1906, was enthralled by the scenery, and took up residence within the present bounds of the monument. By 1907 Otto had decided that these canyons, particularly Monument Canyon, should be a national park. He started a one-man letter-writing campaign to the federal government, advocating protection of the site, and also initiated a petition and rallied local support for the establishment of a public park. His efforts

LEE GREGORY

A mass of sandstone has been eroded into rounded domes that resemble coke ovens.

STATE OF COLORADO

Independence Monument, a 700-foot sandstone fin, stands on the divide between two canyons.

3 COLORADO NATIONAL MONUMENT

were rewarded on May 24, 1911, when President William Howard Taft signed a proclamation establishing Colorado National Monument.

John Otto was the monument's first custodian. He became a prolific trail builder and promoter who wanted everyone to enjoy the scenery of his monument. However, the earliest trails through the park were narrow paths, suitable only for the adventurous. By 1921 Otto had completed the Trail of the Serpent, a road that climbed to the monument's rim over a series of 54 switchbacks. In 1927 he took an interest in a political career and gave up his post as custodian. Some of his original trails along the monument's rim were widened into the modern Rim Rock Drive by the Civilian Conservation Corps during the depression of the 1930s.

Today this road has numerous turnouts that offer views above the monument's many dramatic canyons. Three prominent formations are Balanced Rock, the Coke Ovens, and Independence Monument, a nearly 700-foot tall sandstone fin. Independence Monument is the remnant of a once prominent divide between Monument Canyon to the south and Wedding Canyon to the north. Most of this thin divide collapsed, but Independence Monument remains, perched on a lower, but still functional, divide. Another dramatic stop along Rim Rock Drive is Cold Shivers Point, overlooking a sheer drop of over 300 feet to the floor of Columbus Canyon. The best photo is not from the overlook, but of someone standing at the overlook as seen from the head of Columbus Canyon. Be sure to drive the loop road to the campground. It offers a long view through Monument Canyon and a short walk to Window Rock, a small natural opening. Some of the more remote portions of the monument can be penetrated by foot over a variety of trails. No Thoroughfare Canyon, for example, a large 1979 addition to the monument, offers fine hiking opportunities in a quiet, wilderness environment.

DIRECTIONS: The easiest way to find Colorado National Monument is to take exit 19 <0.0>, the Fruita exit just west of Grand Junction, from Interstate 70. Here, signs direct you toward the monument on Colorado 340. Turn right onto a paved road <2.4> to reach the west entrance station <2.6>. This road, Rim Rock Drive, then climbs to the top of a sandstone rim and follows it for several miles. The paved road passes the campground <6.8>, the visitor center <6.9>, the access road <13.4> to Rattlesnake Canyon (see site 2), the Glade Park Road <21.1> to Miracle Rock (see site 1), and numerous scenic turnouts before descending to the east entrance station <24.9>.

You can also reach the monument from Grand Junction. At the west end of the older downtown business district of Grand Junction, Business Loop 70/US 50/US 6 meets Colorado 340. Signs mark this turn as access to Colorado National Monument. From this junction <0.0>, turn west onto Colorado 340. Follow it a short distance, crossing the Colorado River. A green sign indicates that you should turn left at the stoplight <1.0>. Then follow the paved Monument Road out of town to the east entrance <4.5>.

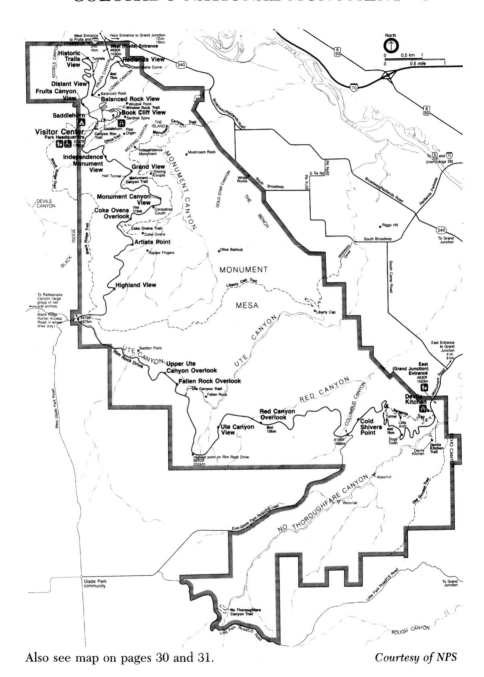

Also see map on pages 30 and 31.   *Courtesy of NPS*

4 MOUNT GARFIELD

TYPE: Plateau Scenery/Geologic
ADMINISTRATION: BLM land/Private land
QUALITY: Scenic
ACCESS: Paved road
FACILITIES: None
TIME NEEDED: Quarter hour
BEST VISIT: Spring or fall
BEST PHOTO: Afternoon to late afternoon
ELEVATION: 6,765 feet
REFERENCE: Palisade
MAP: State highway map
Grand Mesa National Forest visitor map
USGS TOPO: Clifton 7.5' (1973)
USGS COUNTY: Mesa County Sheet 2 of 6 (1975)

Mount Garfield marks the eastern end of the Little Book Cliffs. Extending over 175 miles, these cliffs continue to Price, Utah, where they are called the Big Book Cliffs. The cliffs stand from 1,000 to 2,000 feet tall. Nearly all of this height is Mancos shale, a soft, gray rock that is easily eroded. The top of these cliffs, including Mount Garfield, is capped by a resistant layer of Mesa Verde sandstone. Grand Valley, carpeted with Mancos shale above a base of Dakota sandstone, was cut by the Colorado River, which was known as the Grand River until 1921. The name of Grand Valley was not changed, despite the renaming of the river, and Grand Junction derived its name from the nearby confluence of the Grand and Gunnison rivers.

Mount Garfield and the continuing Little Book Cliffs are both desolate and beautiful. There is virtually no vegetation growing on the cliff face to obscure the geologic view. In 1853 the Book Cliffs were noted by explorer John W. Gunnison who was reminded of a line of upright open volumes, their fanned-out pages facing the desolate valley.

The town of Palisade is named for the formations on the southern face of Mount Garfield. Here, boulders of Mesa Verde sandstone have broken from the rim and lodged in the soft, sloping shale of the cliff face. The sandstone acts as a protective cap against erosion, thus preserving its shale support. The surrounding unprotected shale is easily eroded, resulting in the boulders being supported by a narrow column of shale, detached from the rest of the cliff. Some of these spires, or palisades, rise as much as 60 feet above the remaining slope. The eastern end of Grand Valley, near Palisade, is a fruit-producing region. A desert-like climate and westerly winds that are warmed by compression as they try to enter the funnel-shaped Colorado River Canyon provide an extended growing season.

DIRECTIONS: Proceed west on Interstate 70 from the Palisade exit <0.0> (exit 42) toward Grand Junction. A large turnout <3.3> on the right (north) side of Interstate 70 provides a good view of Mount Garfield.

The gray slopes of Mount Garfield are bare of vegetation.

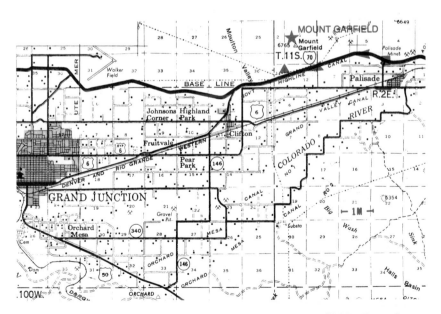

Courtesy of USDA Forest Service

5 GRAND MESA

TYPE:	Plateau Scenery/Geologic
ADMINISTRATION:	Grand Mesa National Forest
QUALITY:	Scenic
ACCESS:	Dirt road
FACILITIES:	Picnic areas/Rest rooms/Nearby campgrounds
TIME NEEDED:	Two hours
BEST VISIT:	Early summer to fall
BEST PHOTO:	Midday
ELEVATION:	9,920 feet (top of Lands End Road)
REFERENCE:	Whitewater
MAP:	State highway map
	Grand Mesa National Forest visitor map
USGS TOPO:	Lands End 7.5' (1962)
USGS COUNTY:	Mesa County Sheet 3 of 6 (1975)
	Delta County Sheet 2 of 3 (1975)

With an area of 53 square miles, Grand Mesa is one of the largest plateaus in the nation. It is also one of the highest. At an elevation of 10,000 feet, it stands a full mile above Grand Valley to the west. The flat surface of the mesa was formed by lava flows 100 to 400 feet thick. The lava rests atop thousands of feet of sedimentary rock of the same variety that has been eroded and removed by the Colorado River to form Grand Valley. The lava has protected Grand Mesa and demonstrates how high the entire region would be, were it not for erosion. Because the lava flows have formed a pitted, flat surface, the mesa top is scattered with over 200 lakes. Grand Mesa was once a favorite hunting ground of the Ute Indians who called it Thigunawat, the home of departed spirits.

Grand Mesa offers fine scenery and recreational opportunities. The forest is particularly beautiful when the aspens turn, usually in late September. There is an overlook at Lands End, one of the most westerly extremes of the mesa. The site is well named, for the level plateau comes to an abrupt edge with a drop of thousands of feet. An incredible road has been built from this rim to the valley below, descending the sloping cliffs by a seemingly endless succession of switchbacks and curves. Lands End Road is an enjoyable passenger car route when dry.

DIRECTIONS: From Grand Junction, follow US 50 south past its junction <0.0> with Colorado 141 at Whitewater. Turn left onto a paved road <4.2> identified by a sign as access to Lands End. Heed a sign <7.1> telling you to keep left. The pavement ends <13.5> at the boundary of Grand Mesa National Forest. Continue on the dirt road as it winds to the rim <25.3> over numerous switchbacks. An observation site is on the left, just at the top of the rim. The road continues east across the flat mesa to Colorado 65 <36.8>. To the left are views into the Colorado River Valley; to the right are overlooks of the many lakes on the mesa top.

LEE GREGORY

A thick volcanic layer forms the flat surface of Grand Mesa.

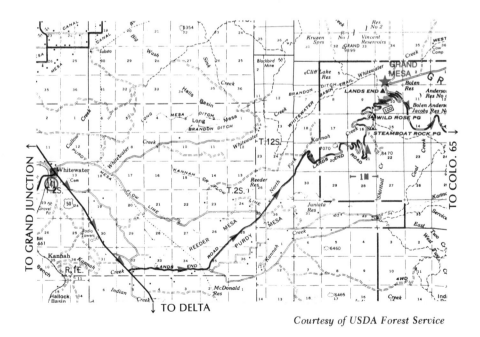

Courtesy of USDA Forest Service

6 UNAWEEP CANYON

TYPE:	Plateau Scenery/Geologic
ADMINISTRATION:	Private land
QUALITY:	Scenic
ACCESS:	Paved road
FACILITIES:	None
TIME NEEDED:	One hour
BEST VISIT:	Spring or fall
BEST PHOTO:	Morning
ELEVATION:	7,048 feet (Unaweep Divide)
REFERENCE:	Whitewater
MAP:	State highway map
	Uncompahgre National Forest visitor map
USGS TOPO:	Snyder Flats 7.5′ (1973)
USGS COUNTY:	Mesa County Sheets 5 and 6 of 6 (1975)

Beautiful Unaweep Canyon is a 2,500-foot deep, mile wide, 40-mile long valley. The gently curved, symmetrical features of the canyon give it the appearance of a retired canyon, and indeed it is. Several geologists suggest the following theory to explain Unaweep's much more active past.

The ancestral Colorado and Gunnison rivers once joined and flowed over soft shale to a junction with the Dolores River, which then flowed into Utah. About eight million years ago, what is now the Uncompahgre Plateau began to lift from beneath the shale. As this uplift progressed, the combined Colorado and Gunnison rivers began to cut Unaweep Canyon through the rising soft sedimentary rocks between Whitewater and Gateway. Eventually the uplift caused a ridge to form between the Colorado and the Gunnison. The Colorado was forced to detour around the Uncompahgre Plateau through Grand Valley to the north. Unaweep had lost the Colorado, but it still carried the Gunnison. Later, the Gunnison was unable to cut through the granite below the sedimentary rocks fast enough to maintain its course. It too joined the Colorado to evade the rising Uncompahgre Plateau.

Unaweep Canyon continued to rise, but without a river. Later, glaciation converted the rough canyon to its present U-shape. The floor of Unaweep is now more than 2,000 feet above the course of the Colorado River at Grand Junction. Two small streams drain the canyon in opposite directions from Unaweep Divide, the high point of the canyon floor.

DIRECTIONS: From Grand Junction follow US 50 south to its junction <0.0> with Colorado 141 at Whitewater. Follow Colorado 141 west into Unaweep Canyon. Continue past the Cactus Park Road <8.9> to the Divide Road <14.3>, marked by a green sign. You may wish to turn left onto this good dirt road and follow it to the rim of Unaweep Canyon for a fine view.

Continue on the paved valley road to Unaweep Divide, marked by a sign <19.7> on the right. From here, the road descends to the west end of Unaweep Canyon just before reaching Gateway <43.1> (see site 7).

LEE GREGORY

U-shaped Unaweep Canyon once carried a major river.

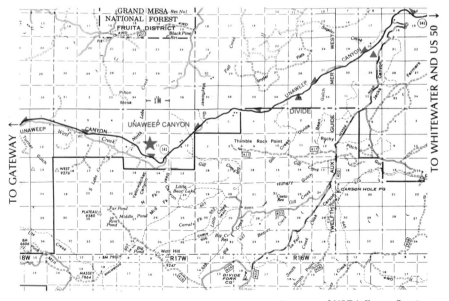

Courtesy of USDA Forest Service

7 DOLORES CANYON

TYPE:	Plateau Scenery/Geologic/Historic
ADMINISTRATION:	BLM land/Private land
QUALITY:	Scenic
ACCESS:	Paved road
FACILITIES:	None
TIME NEEDED:	One hour
BEST VISIT:	Spring or fall
BEST PHOTO:	Midday to afternoon
ELEVATION:	5,150 feet (Hanging Flume Overlook)
REFERENCE:	Uravan
MAP:	State highway map
	Uncompahgre National Forest visitor map
USGS TOPO:	Red Canyon 7.5′ (1960)
USGS COUNTY:	Montrose County Sheet 3 of 4 (1979)
	Mesa County Sheet 5 of 6 (1975)

Dolores Canyon is among Colorado's most scenic and accessible sandstone canyons. As you drive through the canyon, you will pass through various layers of sedimentary rock, including the youngest (top) and the oldest (bottom): light brown Dakota sandstone (road level at the southern end of the canyon); dinosaur fossil-containing red and gray shale of the Morrison formation; uranium-containing red and green mudstone and siltstone of the Summerville formation; slickrock Entrada sandstone; step- and ledge-forming Kayenta matrix; vertical cliff-forming red Wingate sandstone; and sloping bright red Redbeds of the Chinle and Moenkopi formations (road level near Gateway). These layers are part of the Colorado Plateau, which extends west across Utah and south to the Grand Canyon.

This is uranium country. Carnotite, a yellow ore of uranium, was known in the area for years, but there was little use for it until an order came from France. In 1898 several tons of carnotite were mined near Uravan, hauled by mule and wagon to Placerville, and loaded into ore cars of the Rio Grande Southern Railroad. The carnotite was eventually delivered to Pierre and Marie Curie in Paris who refined it to produce radium. A small mill near Uravan was kept busy supplying the demand for radium until 1921. In 1938 a new mill was built at Uravan to extract vanadium, a metal used in steel alloys. Vanadium was processed from carnotite ore until 1940.

In 1941 representatives of the federal government showed up with a quiet interest in the residue of the vanadium milling process. That year the Uravan mill was converted to extract uranium from the carnotite. A considerable amount of uranium was mined from the Dolores Canyon and other mines on the Colorado Plateau and then milled and stored at Uravan. This uranium would fill the needs of the Manhattan Project, the government's top secret atomic bomb development project at Los Alamos, New Mexico, during World War II. There was a lull in uranium mining after 1945 until the U-boom of the 1950s. The boom died out in 1962, but its effects can still be

LEE GREGORY

The remains of the Hanging Flume can still be seen along the wall of the canyon.

LEE GREGORY

A sign gives a short history of the flume.

7 DOLORES CANYON

seen in the numerous mines throughout the Dolores Canyon.

Several local town names reflect the nature of this uranium mining district. The name "Uravan" is a contraction of uranium and vanadium. "Nucla" also sounds like a fitting name for the atomic age, but this town was named long before "nuclear" was an important term. Nucla was organized in 1904 by the Colorado Cooperative Company, a socialistic farm colony. The town was named "Nucla," short for "nucleus," because the members believed their movement would spread, and this would become the center of the socialist world.

Uranium is not the only valuable mineral in the canyon. Gold, washed down from the San Juan Mountains, is found in small amounts in the gravel and sand bars along the Dolores River. A St. Louis based mining company was determined to recover some of this gold on Mesa Creek Flats through hydraulic mining. To raise water to the level of the flats, an incredible flume was built along the walls of the San Miguel and Dolores river canyons. The 6-mile, 4- by 6-foot wooden flume, supplemented by a 7-mile ditch, was started in 1889 and was completed two years later at a cost over $100,000. To construct the flume, workers were lowered as much as 400 feet from the canyon rim or suspended from a frame beyond the unfinished end of the flume. The flume was an engineering success, supplying 80,000,000 gallons of water a day, and a financial disaster. It was discovered that hydraulic mining was ineffective in recovering the gold. The project was a total loss.

DIRECTIONS: From the junction <0.0> of Colorado highways 141 and 145, proceed north on Colorado 141 through the town of Naturita <3.7> toward Uravan, with its uranium processing mill and settling ponds. Continue past Uravan <19.2> where the canyon scenery starts to improve. The San Miguel River joins the Dolores River <24.1>, and you may notice mines above the slickrock of the east canyon wall. A "point of interest" sign <25.2> points to a turnout on the left for a viewpoint of the Hanging Flume.

The road continues through Dolores Canyon, with numerous uranium mines above the interesting slickrock sandstone of the east canyon wall. The road descends to the river level <27.9> and continues through a scenic and colorful portion of the canyon. Spring water is available on the left <28.7>, and the canyon becomes narrow between walls of sheer Wingate sandstone. The slickrock layer is now above this steep Wingate.

A cistern <35.2> is located on the left side of the road to collect spring water. The highway follows the floor of the canyon as it continues to cut deeper through the stratigraphic layers. The canyon begins to open and becomes wide before crossing the Dolores River <54.4> at Gateway. The highway then turns east to pass through Unaweep Canyon (see site 6) on its way to join US 50, just south of Grand Junction.

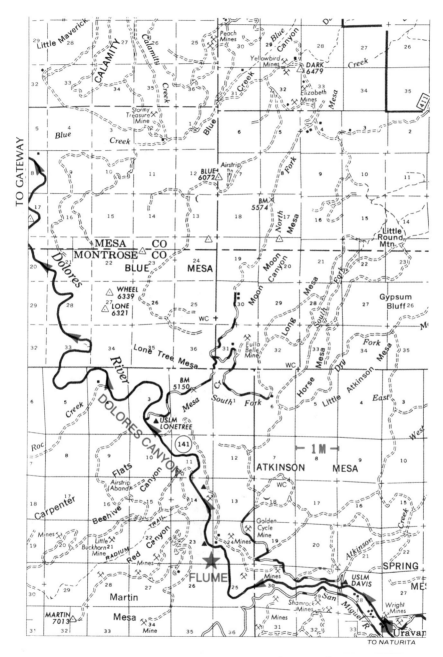

Courtesy of USDA Forest Service

GUNNISON DISTRICT

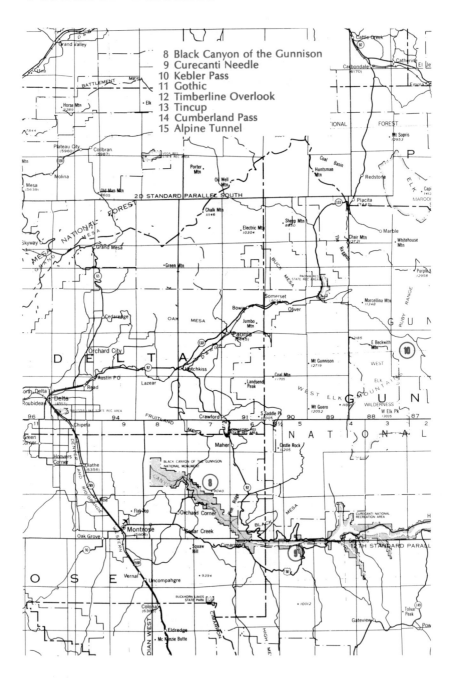

8 Black Canyon of the Gunnison
9 Curecanti Needle
10 Kebler Pass
11 Gothic
12 Timberline Overlook
13 Tincup
14 Cumberland Pass
15 Alpine Tunnel

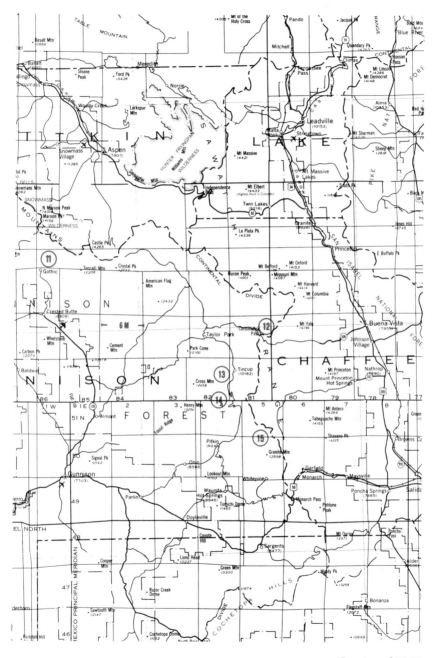

Courtesy of USGS

8 BLACK CANYON OF THE GUNNISON

TYPE: Plateau Scenery/Geologic
ADMINISTRATION: National Monument
QUALITY: Extremely scenic
ACCESS: Paved road (south rim)/Good dirt road (north rim)
FACILITIES: Visitor center/Campgrounds/Picnic areas
TIME NEEDED: Two hours
BEST VISIT: Spring to fall
BEST PHOTO: All day
ELEVATION: 8,160 feet (visitor center)
REFERENCE: Montrose
MAP: State highway map
Gunnison National Forest visitor map
USGS TOPO: Black Canyon of the Gunnison National Monument
USGS COUNTY: Montrose County Sheet 2 of 4 (1979)

No other canyon in America is quite like this one. Other canyons may be deeper, more narrow, steeper, or longer than Black Canyon, but none combines these qualities into a more dramatic defile. The boundaries of the monument enclose the deepest and most spectacular twelve miles of the 53-mile long Black Canyon of the Gunnison River.

The canyon was slowly cut by the river over a period of two million years. The hard, dark walls of the canyon are ancient Precambrian rocks, including platy schist, coarse granite, and gray quartz monzonite. These basement rocks were once covered with layers of sedimentary rocks and volcanic flows; all but a thin veneer atop the rims has been removed by erosion. The course of the river was established on the soft volcanic rock, and once committed, it was obliged to cut into the present canyon's hard, crystalline rocks during the regional uplift.

Today, the depth of the Black Canyon ranges from 1,730 to 2,700 feet. The canyon narrows from 1,300 feet at the rim to as little as 40 feet at the river, which drops an energetic 95 feet per mile. The 2,300-foot Painted Wall is the highest cliff in Colorado and is perhaps the best example of the canyon's geology. The gray to pink bands in the Painted Wall are intrusions of molten granite that squeezed into cracks over a billion years ago.

The Ute Indians were the resident tribe when the Spanish began their explorations of this territory, as in Coronado's search for gold in 1541. Spaniards led by Don Juan Maria de Rivera encountered the Gunnison River near the west end of the canyon in 1765, during their search for gold. In 1853 John W. Gunnison passed through the region but avoided the rugged canyon terrain. The canyon's first partial survey as a possible rail route was made in the winter of 1882-83 by Byron Bryant. In 1901 W. W. Torrence and A. L. Fellows made the first successful trip through the canyon to survey for a possible irrigation tunnel to the Uncompahgre Valley.

The boundaries of the monument, established in 1933 by President Hoover, now enclose 21 square miles of rim and canyon. The south rim drive

LEE GREGORY

The 2,300-foot Painted Wall is the highest cliff in Colorado.

is paved and follows the canyon closely for eight miles with numerous overlooks. The north rim drive is five miles of good graded road also leading to various viewpoints, including the magnificent Long View. The 82-mile drive from rim to rim takes about two hours. The north rim is often closed in the winter because of snow, but the south rim is kept open all year, at least as far as Gunnison Point. There are no trails into the canyon.

DIRECTIONS: From the junction <0.0> of US 50 and Colorado 347 (8 miles east of Montrose), follow Colorado 347 to the south rim <5.5>.

Reaching the north rim is a little more complex. From the junction <0.0> of Colorado highways 133 and 92 in Hotchkiss, follow Colorado 92 through Crawford <10.7> and pass the Crawford Reservoir <12.3> on the right. Turn right onto a gravel road <13.9> marked by a sign as access to Black Canyon of the Gunnison National Monument. This good dirt road goes around the reservoir and then heads south <15.4>. The route now winds through a maze of roads with small brown signs to keep you on course.

Turn left at a junction <16.0> marked by a sign. Continue past a side road <17.9> on the right, and almost immediately thereafter, turn right at an intersection <17.95> marked by a sign. A sign indicates you should turn left at another junction <18.7>. Stay on the main gravel road, marked by a sign <20.6>, as it curves to the right. The road now continues directly over open country to the rim road <25.2>. The campground and ranger station are to the right, and numerous viewpoints are to the left.

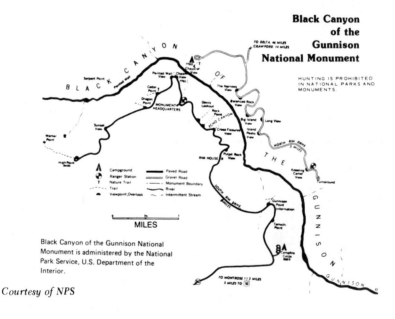

**Black Canyon
of the
Gunnison
National Monument**

HUNTING IS PROHIBITED
IN NATIONAL PARKS AND
MONUMENTS.

MILES

Black Canyon of the Gunnison National
Monument is administered by the National
Park Service, U.S. Department of the
Interior.

Courtesy of NPS

Courtesy of USDA Forest Service

9 CURECANTI NEEDLE

TYPE: Plateau Scenery/Geologic/Historic
ADMINISTRATION: Curecanti National Recreation Area
QUALITY: Scenic
ACCESS: Paved road
FACILITIES: Rest rooms/Nearby campgrounds and picnic areas
TIME NEEDED: Half hour
BEST VISIT: Spring to fall
BEST PHOTO: Morning or afternoon
ELEVATION: 7,856 feet
REFERENCE: Sapinero
MAP: State highway map
Gunnison National Forest visitor map
USGS TOPO: Curecanti Needle 7.5' (1956)
USGS COUNTY: Gunnison County Sheet 4 of 6 (1976)

Curecanti Needle became a famous scenic attraction after the Denver and Rio Grande Railroad laid tracks through the upper Black Canyon of the Gunnison River and started carrying regular passenger traffic on this route in 1882. The needle is mentioned and is often sketched in a number of late 1800s publications that describe the scenery along this branch. The name "Curecanti" originally belonged to a Ute Indian who directed the Ute Bear Dance with his twin brother during annual spring festivals.

The needle is an 800-foot, pyramid-like spire separated from the 1,000-foot canyon walls surrounding it at the confluence of Blue Creek and the Gunnison River. The appearance of the needle from the railroad grade must have been enhanced by the already dramatic confines of the canyon. This part of the canyon was inundated by the Morrow Point Reservoir as it filled behind the dam that was begun in 1963 by the Bureau of Reclamation.

The most practical way to view the needle today is from the north rim of the canyon. State Highway 92 follows the old Black Mesa Indian Trail along this rim between Blue Mesa Dam and Black Mesa, west of the needle. A short road marked by a sign leads from the highway to Pioneer Point, almost directly across from the needle. This overlook is dedicated to the memory of all western Colorado pioneers. Another good vantage point is about a mile east of Pioneer Point on the highway, where a bend in the river allows an unobstructed view of the needle framed by the narrow slice of the canyon.

Another overlook worth mentioning is along Colorado 92 near Cimarron Point, about 11 miles west of Pioneer Point. From here are views of Morrow Point Dam, its reservoir, and the San Juan Mountains far to the south. The entire highway along this north rim is scenic and provides several good views of the upper Black Canyon of the Gunnison.

DIRECTIONS: From the junction <0.0> of US 50 and Colorado 92, follow Colorado 92 across Blue Mesa Dam <0.7> to the parking area at Pioneer Point (Curecanti Needle Overlook) <6.0>, identified by a sign.

LEE GREGORY

Curecanti Needle, 800 feet tall, stands apart from the left side of the canyon.

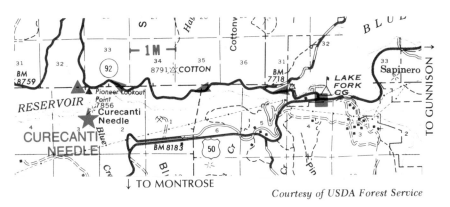

Courtesy of USDA Forest Service

10 KEBLER PASS

TYPE: Mountain Scenery/Historic
ADMINISTRATION: Gunnison National Forest
QUALITY: Very scenic
ACCESS: Good dirt road
FACILITIES: Campgrounds
TIME NEEDED: Two hours
BEST VISIT: Early summer to fall
BEST PHOTO: Morning
ELEVATION: 10,007 feet
REFERENCE: Crested Butte
MAP: State highway map
Gunnison National Forest visitor map
USGS TOPO: Mount Axtell 7.5' (1973)
USGS COUNTY: Gunnison County Sheet 2 of 6 (1976)

Kebler Pass Road (Colorado 135 on some maps) is a scenic connection between Crested Butte and the Paonia Reservoir, near Colorado 133 to the west. It offers many fine views into the surrounding West Elk Mountains, and it passes the sites of several old mining towns. The road also passes through thick stands of large aspens which are spectacular when they turn—usually in late September. The West Elk Wilderness lies to the south, and the Ruby Range to the north shows numerous mining scars.

Kebler Pass, one of Colorado's more gentle crossings, was named in honor of J. A. Kebler, an associate of John C. Osgood who was well-known for his coal mines at Redstone. Kebler Pass Road follows the route of an old, but once well used, Ute Indian trail. Between Kebler Pass and Crested Butte the road also generally follows the abandoned grade of the Crested Butte Branch of the Denver and Rio Grande Railroad. The wide, well-graded road makes a pleasant drive for passenger cars.

Just north of Kebler Pass, at the shore of Lake Irwin, with a fine view of the Ruby Range to the west, is the site of Irwin, a famous Gunnison County mining camp. The first strike was made in June 1879. Dick Irwin, an early prospector, sent an ore sample to Denver to be assayed. The secret of Irwin's find was out. Soon there were numerous prospectors exploring and camping here, and despite this being Ute land, a town was built. The threat of Indian attack was a constant fear, but none materialized.

Irwin peaked in 1882. The town's main street, a mile long, was lined with numerous businesses, including a bank, a theater, many hotels and shops, and a weekly newspaper, the *Pilot*. The town also held three churches, six sawmills, a large ore mill, a school, the usual saloons and gambling houses, and a sturdy jail, complete with a pair of marshals who stayed busy. Former President Ulysses S. Grant spent two days in Irwin in 1880 and was lavishly entertained at the exclusive Irwin Club. The town died almost as suddenly as it began and was deserted by 1885. Today, there is little left except the old Irwin cemetery to remind us that there had ever been a town.

Lake Irwin forms a reflecting surface for the Ruby Range.

The West Elk Mountains are just south of the Kebler Pass Road.

10   KEBLER PASS

DIRECTIONS: From Crested Butte, proceed west on the town's main street (Elk Avenue) to its end <0.0>. Turn left and follow First Street to a junction <0.4>with White Rock Avenue. Turn right and follow the road west as it heads up the valley, away from town. Ignore a side road <2.1> on the right which is an access to the Mount Emmons project, a possible molybdenum mine site. Continue past the Gunnison National Forest boundary sign <2.2> to the junction with a side road <6.7> on the right. You may wish to turn right and then left at the next fork to visit beautiful Lake Irwin.

Continuing on the main road, you come to a junction <7.1> with a side road on the left, marked by a sign that indicates left for the Ohio Pass Road and right for the Kebler Pass Road. The Ohio Pass Road crosses Ohio Pass (2 miles) on its way toward Gunnison (26 miles). Bear right and continue to

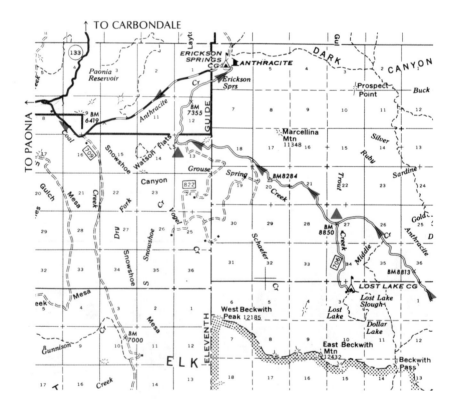

Kebler Pass <7.3>, marked on the left (south) by a sign. To the right (north), at the very top of the pass, is the old Irwin cemetery.

Continuing on the main road, cross a small bridge <9.1> with a good view to the west and continue past a side road <16.5> on the left, marked by a sign as access to Lost Lake Campground and resort (nice view to the left). The road passes through a choice segment of aspen forest <17.7> before it winds around the base of a large, serrated mountain, north of the road. The route passes through another stand of aspen <21.1> and offers additional views <22.1> of the West Elk Mountains. After another fine vista <25.0> to the north, the road descends to a bridge <25.7> at Erickson Springs Campground. Continue past the Gunnison National Forest Boundary <26.1>. The road ends at a T-intersection <31.9> with Colorado 133. To the right are Paonia Reservoir, Marble, and Redstone; to the left are Paonia, Hotchkiss, and Delta.

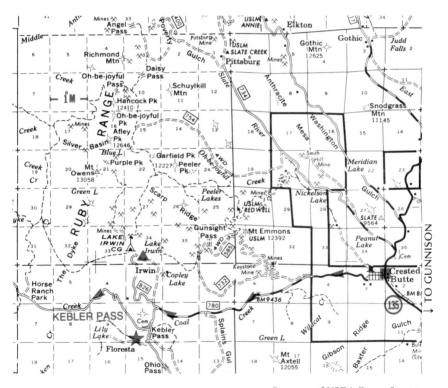

Courtesy of USDA Forest Service

11 GOTHIC

TYPE:	Mountain Scenery/Historic
ADMINISTRATION:	Private land
QUALITY:	Very scenic
ACCESS:	Good dirt road
FACILITIES:	Nearby campgrounds and picnic areas
TIME NEEDED:	One hour
BEST VISIT:	Early summer to fall
BEST PHOTO:	Afternoon
ELEVATION:	9,470 feet
REFERENCE:	Crested Butte
MAP:	State highway map
	Gunnison National Forest visitor map
USGS TOPO:	Gothic 7.5′ (1961)
USGS COUNTY:	Gunnison County Sheet 2 of 6 (1976)

In the fall of 1878 Truman Blancett wandered into this valley of the Elk Mountains and prospected a few hundred dollars worth of silver. Such secrets were hard to keep, and there were hundreds prospecting in the valley when he returned the next spring. Gothic was the largest and wildest Gunnison County camp during the 1880s. Some of the best ores assayed at $15,000 per ton. The 1880 census showed a population of 950, but some say that the count later increased to 8,000.

The biggest event in Gothic's history was the 1880 visit of former President Ulysses S. Grant who was greeted with a lively parade. By the 1890s everyone had left Gothic except Garwood Judd, the last mayor of Gothic. Judd was the only town resident until his death in 1930. About that time, the townsite was purchased for $200 by John C. Johnston who was starting the Rocky Mountain Biological Laboratory. This site was an ideal location for the study of high altitude flora and fauna. Some of the nation's first ecologists studied here. Today, the privately owned buildings of Gothic are maintained by the biological laboratory.

Gothic rests in one of the most beautiful mountain valleys in Colorado. While visiting Gothic, please stay on the main street as the town is privately owned. You may wish to continue north to enjoy the valley's scenery. There are two campgrounds and a picnic area along the road to Scofield Pass. If you want to cross this pass, however, a four-wheel-drive vehicle is required.

DIRECTIONS: From Crested Butte <0.0> go north on the paved road (Gunnison County 317) that continues from Colorado 135. Pass through Mount Crested Butte and continue on the main road through the ski resort to the end of the pavement <3.8>. Continue north on the gravel road and pass the Gunnison National Forest sign <4.4> on the way to Gothic <7.8>. You can continue through Gothic to enjoy the scenery north of town. This road eventually becomes a jeep road.

LEE GREGORY

The buildings of Gothic are in a spectacular mountain valley.

Courtesy of USDA Forest Service

12 TIMBERLINE OVERLOOK

TYPE: Mountain Scenery
ADMINISTRATION: Gunnison National Forest
QUALITY: Scenic
ACCESS: Good dirt road
FACILITIES: Rest rooms
TIME NEEDED: Half hour
BEST VISIT: Midsummer to late summer
BEST PHOTO: Morning
ELEVATION: 12,040 feet
REFERENCE: Buena Vista
MAP: State highway map
Gunnison National Forest visitor map
USGS TOPO: Mount Harvard 15' (1955)
USGS COUNTY: Gunnison County Sheet 3 of 6 (1976)

Timberline Overlook provides a fine view of the Sawatch Range, which forms both the northern and eastern boundaries of Taylor Park, and of Taylor Park itself, stretching northwest toward Aspen. The slopes around the overlook are a good place to see mountain flowers that prefer an alpine climate. These wildflowers are often at their peak from the end of July through mid-August. This is a particularly good spot to find Colorado Columbine, the state flower.

Cottonwood Pass (12,126 feet), a Continental Divide crossing, is just east of the overlook. The pass, one of the highest automobile crossings in Colorado, offers broad views of both the Atlantic and Pacific watersheds of the Sawatch Range.

The history of the Cottonwood Pass Road—like most pass roads in Colorado—began as a result of great mineral wealth. The mining boom of the late 1870s in the Gunnison district, as well as points north, south, and west, posed the need for a transportation route from the Arkansas Valley to the western slope of the Continental Divide. A toll road was completed over Cottonwood Pass in 1880 which served the mining activities in Tincup, Pitkin, and Gunnison. It was also the major connection to Ashcroft and Aspen by means of Taylor Pass. This freighting route served a vast mining region but was short-lived. The toll company operating the road went bankrupt in 1882, leaving the county as the new owner. The Forest Service constructed a new route over Cottonwood Pass in 1960.

DIRECTIONS: From the junction <0.0> of US 24 and Colorado 306 in Buena Vista, follow Colorado 306 west toward Cottonwood Pass <19.2>, marked by a sign as a Continental Divide crossing. Continue beyond the pass to a sign <20.3> that marks the turn for the Timberline Overlook parking area. Climb the hill behind the parking area for good views to the north. The main road continues west to Taylor Park Reservoir <32.7> (see site 13).

LEE GREGORY

The Continental Divide follows the Sawatch Range along the north wall of Taylor Park.

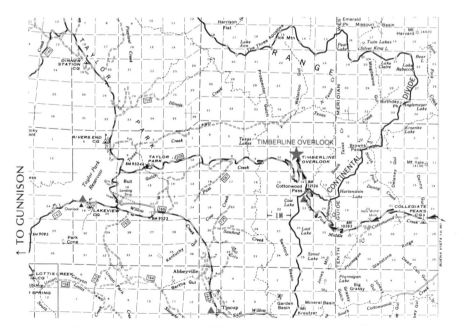

Also see map on pages 68 and 69.   *Courtesy of USDA Forest Service*

13 TINCUP

TYPE:	Mountain Scenery/Historic
ADMINISTRATION:	Private land
QUALITY:	Scenic
ACCESS:	Good dirt road
FACILITIES:	Nearby campground
TIME NEEDED:	Half hour
BEST VISIT:	Early summer to fall
BEST PHOTO:	Morning to midday
ELEVATION:	10,160 feet
REFERENCE:	Tincup
MAP:	State highway map
	Gunnison National Forest visitor map
USGS TOPO:	Mount Harvard 15′ (1955)
USGS COUNTY:	Gunnison County Sheet 3 of 6 (1976)

Many Colorado mining camps have quaint names. Tincup got its when a local miner was seen carrying his hoard of gold dust in a tin cup. Some mineral exploration took place in the area as early as 1859, but it was a rich find in 1879 that started the boom. Tincup was incorporated the following year and peaked in 1882. Tincup was the major supplier of silver in the region, despite the fact that it was never served by a railroad. Ore had to be hauled by mule or wagon to the nearest railhead, which got a little closer each year but never quite made it to town. There was a lull in the mid-1880s, then a resurgence, only to be followed by the recession of the 1893 silver panic. Another rush brought the town back to life in 1902. Afterward, mining subsided although various mines were worked sporadically until the 1930s.

Many believe that Tincup was one of Colorado's three roughest mining towns; Leadville and Creede (see site 38) are popular nominations for the other two positions. Seven Tincup marshals were killed in the span of just a few months, and gun battles were common events. The town was largely controlled by gangsters who appointed corrupt officials.

Tincup was a regional center for supplies and services, having a few mills and smelters, several hotels, numerous stores, a few sawmills, three doctors, a school, the usual saloons and gambling establishments, several newspapers, and a city hall that resembled a church. Tincup was also a social center; miners from all over the district would gather here on weekends for gambling, drinking, and other "sporting" events. Many weathered the winter here, returning to their claims in the spring.

Today most of Tincup's buildings are occupied, and they are all privately owned. The town hall, a church-like structure in the center of town, has been restored, and many of the town's cabins serve as vacation residences. The road leading east out of town goes to a campground on the rim of beautiful Mirror Lake. Beyond the campground, the road becomes a rough jeep trail, crossing Tincup Pass on the way to Saint Elmo.

LEE GREGORY

Tincup's original town hall has been partially restored.

13 TINCUP

DIRECTIONS: There are several good dirt roads leading to Tincup. From the junction <0.0> of US 24 and Colorado 306 in Buena Vista, proceed west on Colorado 306 to Cottonwood Pass <19.2> (see directions for site 12). Continue on the Cottonwood Pass Road to its junction <32.7> with the Taylor Park Road at the east shore of the Taylor Park Reservoir. Here a sign indicates a left turn for Tincup (10 miles). After you turn left, follow the Taylor Park Road to its junction <34.9> with the Cumberland Pass Road, marked by a sign indicating a turn for Tincup (8 miles). Turn left onto the Cumberland Pass Road (Forest Route 765) and follow it to its junction <36.6> with the Willow Creek road (marked by a sign) on the right. Turn left to stay on the Cumberland Pass Road and follow it to Tincup <42.3>.

From Gunnison Tincup can be reached without crossing a pass and with a minimum of dirt road. From the intersection of US 50 and Colorado 135 in Gunnison, head north on Colorado 135 for 10 miles to Almont, where a sign indicates a turn for the Taylor River Road, Taylor Park, and Buena Vista. Turn right and follow the Taylor River Road for another 23 miles to the Taylor Park Reservoir. Follow the road east along the southern shore of the reservoir to its junction with the Cumberland Pass Road. Turn right and follow the Cumberland Pass Road to Tincup.

Tincup can also be reached from the south. From the summit of Cumberland Pass <0.0> (see directions for site 14), continue north on the Cumberland Pass Road. This good dirt road descends through tight switchbacks to reach Tincup <8.5>.

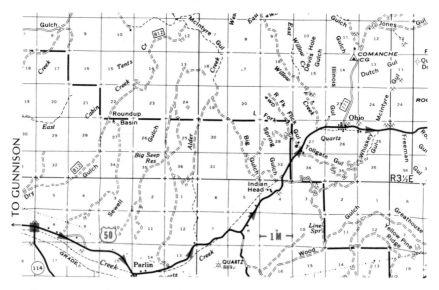

Also see maps on pages 65 and 74.

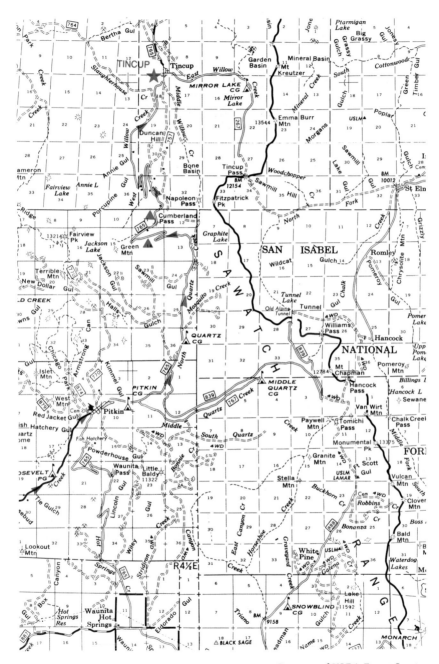

Courtesy of USDA Forest Service

14   CUMBERLAND PASS

TYPE: Mountain Scenery/Historic
ADMINISTRATION: Gunnison National Forest/Private land
QUALITY: Scenic
ACCESS: Good dirt road
FACILITIES: Nearby campgrounds
TIME NEEDED: One hour
BEST VISIT: Midsummer to late summer
BEST PHOTO: Morning
ELEVATION: 12,000 feet
REFERENCE: Pitkin
MAP: State highway map
Gunnison National Forest visitor map
USGS TOPO: Garfield 15' (1940)
USGS COUNTY: Gunnison County Sheet 5 of 6 (1976)

Cumberland Pass, crossed by a good dirt road, is one of the highest passes in Colorado that can be negotiated by passenger car. From the summit you can enjoy impressive vistas into the surrounding Sawatch Range. To the north is the broad expanse of Taylor Park, rimmed by high peaks. To the south is the cozy Quartz Creek Valley, and only two miles to the east is the Continental Divide. The pass itself is fairly colorful—the orange hues result from iron oxides in the light-colored rock.

Local mining activity began in the 1870s, with finds north near Tincup and south along Quartz Creek. In 1880 a pack trail was built across Cumberland Pass to connect these two areas. The trail saw little use, as the Tincup miners found it cheaper to haul their ore over Tincup Pass to Saint Elmo or over Cottonwood Pass (see site 12) to Buena Vista. In 1882 the Cumberland Pass trail was widened into a road, which then saw use because the Denver, South Park and Pacific Railroad had reached Quartz Creek that same year through the Alpine Tunnel (see site 15). The road made mining more attractive at the pass, and you can still see the remains of the Bon Ton Mine on the southern side and the Jimmy Mack Mine on the northern side.

DIRECTIONS: From the junction <0.0> of US 50 and Colorado 114 east of Gunnison, proceed east on US 50 to a side road <3.5> on the left, marked by a large green sign as the road to Ohio City and Pitkin. Turn left and follow this paved road through Ohio City <12.0> to the end of the pavement <18.3> in Pitkin. Continue on the good dirt road that leads north out of Pitkin and ignore the side roads on the right that lead to the Middle Quartz Creek Campground <20.0> and to the Alpine Tunnel <21.5> (see site 15). Continue past Quartz Campground <22.5> and past a side road <23.3> on the left to Halls Gulch and Fairview Peak. The Bon Ton Mine <26.7> is at the base of the switchbacks leading to the summit <29.5> of Cumberland Pass. From here, the road descends to Tincup <38.0> (see site 13).

The remains of the Bon Ton Mine are at the southern base of Cumberland Pass.

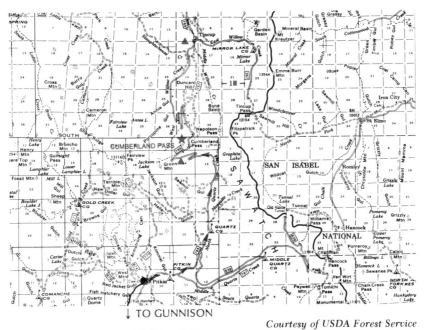

↓ TO GUNNISON

Courtesy of USDA Forest Service

Also see maps on pages 65, 74 and 75.

15 ALPINE TUNNEL

TYPE: Mountain Scenery/Historic
ADMINISTRATION: Gunnison National Forest
QUALITY: Scenic
ACCESS: Rough dirt road
FACILITIES: Rest rooms/Nearby campgrounds
TIME NEEDED: One hour
BEST VISIT: Midsummer to late summer
BEST PHOTO: Midday
ELEVATION: 11,521 feet (west portal)
REFERENCE: Pitkin
MAP: State highway map
Gunnison National Forest visitor map
USGS TOPO: Garfield 15' (1940)
USGS COUNTY: Gunnison County Sheet 5 of 6 (1976)
Chaffee County Sheet 3 of 3 (1980)

The Alpine Tunnel, an incredible piece of railroad engineering, was constructed during 1880-81 by the Denver, South Park and Pacific Railroad. The 1,771-foot long tunnel was bored under the Continental Divide in just 18 months. The work, continuing even in winter, was so demanding that most men stayed on the job only a few weeks. The tunnel needed a construction crew of only 400 at a time, despite a turnover in the labor force of more than 10,000 men. Because of the fierce winter conditions, the tunnel was expensive to maintain. The tunnel was used from 1881 to 1890 and again from 1895 to 1910 when the line was abandoned.

Today the Alpine Tunnel can be reached from either side of the Divide. From the west a narrow, rough dirt road follows the old railroad grade from Quartz Creek to the west portal. A passenger car with good ground clearance and a careful driver can usually make it. Along this route you will pass the Midway and Gulch water tanks. The Midway Tank is in ruins, but the Gulch Tank was restored in 1969. Next you reach the site of Woodstock which had a boardinghouse for the train crews, a telegraph station, a coal platform, and a water tank. Thirteen people were killed when Woodstock was destroyed by an avalanche on March 10, 1884. The Gulch Tank was built to replace the tank lost here.

The grade makes a wide turn at Sherrod Loop and begins the climb to the Palisades which were built to support the tracks along the face of a sheer cliff. The main section is 452 feet long and 33 feet high. The stone retaining wall, which is two feet thick, is made of locally cut stone. Each block was hand-fitted: no mortar was used and yet hardly a stone has been displaced in over 100 years. The grade next crosses the Williams Pass Road which served as a supply route during the construction of the tunnel. The Williams Pass Road is so treacherous that it is now closed even to four-wheel-drive vehicles. Next stop is the west portal. Here, there are the remains of a two-story boarding-house that collapsed in 1958, a stone engine house (rest rooms nearby), a

The old railroad grade is now the road that climbs from Middle Quartz Creek to the west portal of the tunnel.

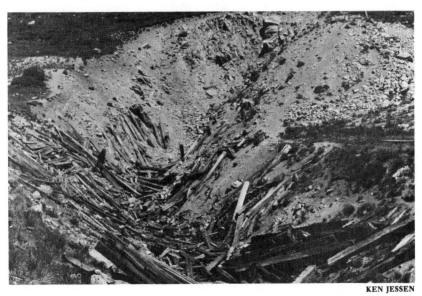

The Alpine Tunnel's west portal is now collapsed.

15 ALPINE TUNNEL

turntable, and the still standing tunnel station (restored in 1959). The west tunnel entrance has now collapsed.

There is little to see at the east portal except another collapsed tunnel entrance and pleasant views to the east. From the east side of the Divide you can drive on good dirt roads to within hiking distance (2¾ miles) of the east portal (11,497 feet), and a trail (about a mile) over Altman (sometimes called Alpine) Pass (11,940 feet) will get you to the west portal.

DIRECTIONS: From the junction <0.0> of US 50 and Colorado 114 east of Gunnison, proceed east on US 50 to a side road <3.5> on the left, marked by a large green sign as the road to Ohio City and Pitkin. Turn left and follow this paved road through Ohio City <12.0> to the end of the pavement <18.3> in Pitkin. Continue on the good dirt road that leads north out of Pitkin, and ignore the side road <20.0> on the right that leads to the Middle Quartz Creek Campground.

A sign marks the road <21.5> on the right as access to the Alpine Tunnel. Turn right and continue on this rough dirt road as it follows the old railroad grade to the tunnel. Continue past the Midway Tank <24.8>, the Gulch Tank <28.1>, and Woodstock <28.7>, each marked by a sign. Follow the road as it makes a wide curve to the left at Sherrod Loop (sign); ignore the side road <29.2> on the right, coming from Hancock Pass. Continue over

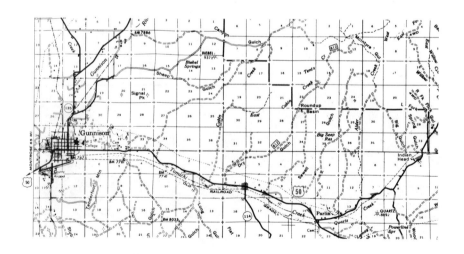

the Palisades <29.6>, and pass the Williams Pass Road sign <30.0> to reach the west portal of the tunnel <31.8>.

An alternative approach to the Alpine Tunnel is from the east side of the Continental Divide. From the junction <0.0> of Colorado 162 and US 285 just south of Buena Vista, follow Colorado 162, which becomes Chaffee County 162 (a good dirt road), west almost to Saint Elmo (see site 38 in *Colorado Scenic Guide: Northern Region*) to a marked side road <15.6> on the left that leads to Hancock. Turn left and follow this good dirt road to Hancock <21.3>, a ghost town. From here, you must hike (or jeep) the remaining 2¾ miles to the tunnel. Follow the nearly level railroad grade (still has ties in a few places) as it leaves northwest from Hancock. From the east portal a trail leads over Altman Pass to the west portal.

Courtesy of USDA Forest Service

FOUR CORNERS DISTRICT

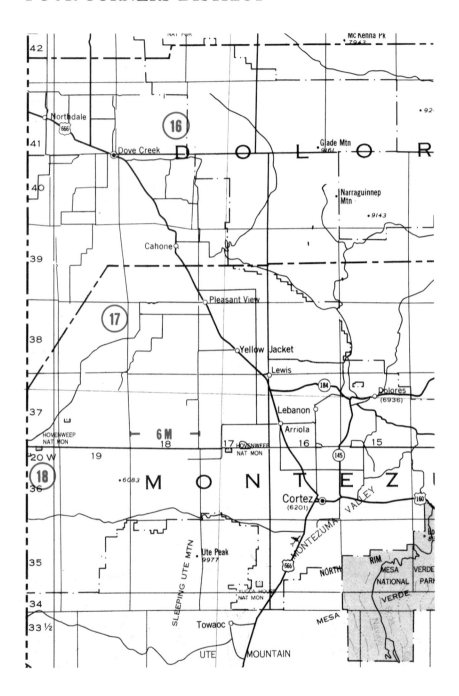

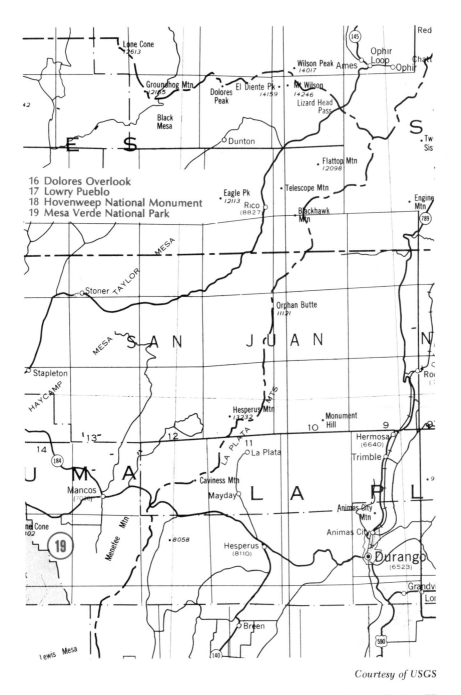

16 Dolores Overlook
17 Lowry Pueblo
18 Hovenweep National Monument
19 Mesa Verde National Park

Courtesy of USGS

16 DOLORES OVERLOOK

TYPE: Plateau Scenery/Geologic
ADMINISTRATION: BLM land
QUALITY: Scenic
ACCESS: Good dirt road
FACILITIES: Picnic area/Rest rooms
TIME NEEDED: Half hour
BEST VISIT: Spring to fall
BEST PHOTO: Midday to afternoon
ELEVATION: 8,000 feet
REFERENCE: Dove Creek
MAP: San Juan National Forest visitor map
USGS TOPO: Secret Canyon 7.5' (1964)
USGS COUNTY: Dolores County Sheet 1 of 3 (1976)

Dolores Overlook is located on a peninsula of land protruding into the deep canyon of the Dolores River as it makes a sweeping U-shaped turn. The river, over 1,000 feet below, was originally named El Rio de Nuestra Señora de los Dolores, the River of Our Lady of Sorrows, by Spanish explorers in the mid-1700s. In 1776 the Dominguez-Escalante Expedition, led by Franciscan Fathers Atanasio Dominguez and Silvestre Velez de Escalante, passed near here on their journey in search of a convenient route from Santa Fe, New Mexico, to the Spanish settlements and missions of California. The party headed northwest into Dolores Canyon, but after several days of difficult and limited progress, they turned back. A Ute guide later led the expedition along an easier route just west of the canyon. They never reached California but were the first Europeans to explore the vast American Southwest.

Dolores Canyon is cut through the sedimentary layers of the Colorado Plateau, and its walls and rim are covered by a thin growth of juniper and pinyon pine. The river drops a swift 25 feet per mile through the canyon below. Upstream, the McPhee Dam, just north of the town of Dolores, regulates the flow through this section of the canyon. It is possible to hike through sections of this canyon.

DIRECTIONS: From the junction <0.0> of US 666 and Colorado 141 just north of Dove Creek, proceed south on US 666 through Dove Creek <2.3> to an intersection <2.9> with a side road, marked by a sign as access to Dolores Canyon Overlook. Turn left onto this good dirt road and continue past an intersecting road <3.1>. Ignore the side roads as the main road curves left <5.3> and then right <5.5>. Later, go straight at an intersection <7.3> where the main road goes to the right. You soon pass a Bureau of Land Management San Juan Resource Area sign. Turn left at a junction <9.7> marked by a sign for the Dolores Canyon Overlook Picnic Ground (3¼ miles). Ignoring the side roads, go straight on this road to the overlook <13.2>.

The Dolores River passes through this canyon over 1,000 feet below.

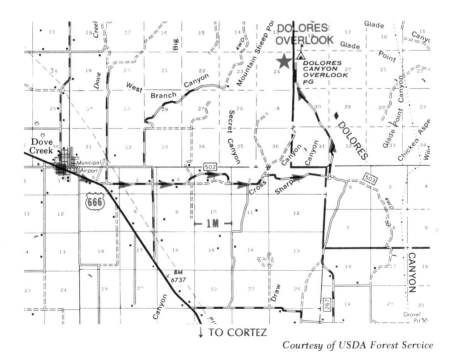

↓ TO CORTEZ

Courtesy of USDA Forest Service

17 LOWRY PUEBLO

TYPE:	Plateau Scenery/Archaeologic
ADMINISTRATION:	BLM land
QUALITY:	Very scenic
ACCESS:	Good dirt road
FACILITIES:	Picnic area/Rest rooms
TIME NEEDED:	One hour
BEST VISIT:	Spring or fall
BEST PHOTO:	Morning or afternoon
ELEVATION:	6,730 feet
REFERENCE:	Pleasant View
MAP:	State highway map
	BLM Dove Creek 1:100,000
USGS TOPO:	Ruin Canyon 7.5' (1979)
USGS COUNTY:	Montezuma County Sheet 1 of 4 (1975)

Lowry Pueblo, named for a local homesteader, was constructed by the Anasazi Indians about A.D. 1090 atop the pithouses of their earlier eighth-century culture. The pueblo's inhabitants were farmers who raised corn, beans, and squash and supplemented their diet by hunting. They also worked stone and made beautifully decorated pottery.

A community of 100 Indians used this site for living quarters and religious ceremonies. Lowry contains one of the largest Great Kivas, a circular ceremonial chamber, yet discovered. The main ruins once stood three stories high, containing 40 rooms and eight smaller kivas. The pueblo was occupied for about 50 years and then abandoned around A.D. 1140 for some unknown reason. The Anasazi probably left in a leisurely manner since no evidence of attack, violence, fire, or other disorder has been discovered.

One of the uniquely preserved features of Lowry is the Painted Kiva, built about 1103. It was decorated with murals, and at least five layers of painted plaster cover its walls. This kiva, with its entrance in the roof, was filled with dirt to support another kiva built on top about 1110. This fill helped to protect the painted plaster, now on display after excavation.

Lowry started as a small village of a few rooms and two kivas. More rooms were added between 1090 and 1103, and further construction between 1103 and 1110 included the Great Kiva. The last remodeling took place about A.D. 1120. The ruins were first excavated in 1928. Restoration began in 1965, and Lowry Pueblo was dedicated as a National Historic Landmark in 1967. Please help preserve this site by not disturbing the ruins. Overnight camping is not allowed.

DIRECTIONS: In the middle of Pleasant View on US 666, a sign marks the side road <0.0> to Lowry Ruins (9 miles). Head west on this paved road which later becomes a good dirt road; ignore all side roads. After a slight curve to the left, turn left onto a side road <8.4>, identified as access to Lowry Ruin, to reach the parking area <8.6>.

LEE GREGORY

Sleeping Ute Mountain rests behind the ruins of Lowry Pueblo.

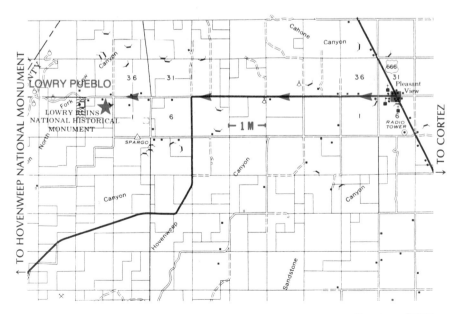

Courtesy of BLM

18 HOVENWEEP NATIONAL MONUMENT

TYPE: Plateau Scenery/Archaeologic
ADMINISTRATION: National Monument
QUALITY: Very scenic
ACCESS: Dirt road
FACILITIES: Visitor center/Campground/Picnic areas
TIME NEEDED: Two hours
BEST VISIT: Spring or fall
BEST PHOTO: Morning or afternoon
ELEVATION: 5,240 feet (visitor center)
REFERENCE: Pleasant View
MAP: State highway map
BLM Cortez 1:100,000
USGS TOPO: Cajon Mesa, Utah-Colorado 15' (1958)
USGS COUNTY: Montezuma County Sheet 1 of 4 (1975)

Pioneer photographer William Henry Jackson was among the first to record the name "Hovenweep" (a Ute Indian word meaning "deserted valley") to describe the region of ruins he photographed in 1874. The Smithsonian Institution made an archaeological survey of the site in 1917-18 and recommended that the ruins be made a national monument. Six groups of ruins, characterized by sqare, round, oval, or D-shaped masonry towers, are now part of Hovenweep National Monument.

The builders of Hovenweep were Anasazi, a farming and hunting culture that inhabited the Four Corners region of Colorado, Utah, New Mexico, and Arizona from nearly 2,000 years ago to about A.D. 1300. Between 1100 and 1200 the local Anasazi gathered from small, scattered villages into towns. They built multistory pueblos at the heads of the Hovenweep canyons which contained permanent springs. Their towers may have been constructed to defend these springs, but there are no signs of violence. It is believed that prolonged drought forced abandonment of the site around A.D. 1300.

The monument's headquarters are located in Utah at the largest and best preserved group of ruins, Square Tower Ruins. The outlying sites include the Cajon Ruins in Utah and the Holly, Hackberry Canyon, Cutthroat Castle, and Goodman Point ruins in Colorado. Please stop at the visitor center (open daily, 8:00 AM to 5:00 PM) for information and directions before visiting the outlying ruins; the Park Service records visitation.

DIRECTIONS: From Pleasant View<0.0>, proceed south on US 666 to a side road <0.8> on the right, marked by a large brown sign identifying this turn for Hovenweep National Monument. Turn right and continue west on this good dirt road. Turn left at an intersecting road <6.8> with a sign indicating Hovenweep National Monument on the left corner. Ignoring the numerous side roads, follow the main dirt road (may be subject to mud after heavy rains) to the Utah state line <23.3>. Continue into Utah to the entrance <26.8>.

U.S. DEPARTMENT OF INTERIOR, NATIONAL PARK SERVICE

These ancient masonry towers were built at the heads of canyons containing springs.

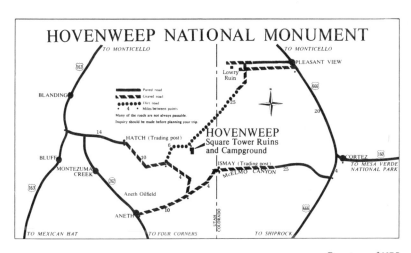

Courtesy of NPS

19 MESA VERDE NATIONAL PARK

TYPE: Plateau Scenery/Archaeologic
ADMINISTRATION: National Park
QUALITY: Extremely scenic
ACCESS: Paved road
FACILITIES: Visitor center/Campground/Picnic areas
TIME NEEDED: Eight hours
BEST VISIT: Spring or fall
BEST PHOTO: All day
ELEVATION: 8,040 feet (visitor center)
REFERENCE: Cortez
MAP: State highway map
San Juan National Forest visitor map
USGS TOPO: Mesa Verde National Park (1967) 1:24,000
USGS COUNTY: Montezuma County Sheet 4 of 4 (1975)

Mesa Verde, Spanish for "green table," was the name given by Spanish explorers who entered southwestern Colorado in the mid-1700s. Even though they named the mesa, they did not explore it. This flat-topped plateau, rising about 2,000 feet above the surrounding Montezuma Valley, is 15 miles long, 8 miles wide, and is cut by numerous finger canyons that provide drainage to the south. Most of the mesa rests atop a thick layer of Mancos shale which is capped with an erosion-resistant layer of Cliff House sandstone. In this upper layer, just below the surface, an impermeable layer of shale forces ground water to move horizontally, rather than just deeper into the earth. The water emerges as seeps and springs just below the rim of many canyons. Over the centuries, this moisture has weakened the sandstone, thus encouraging the formation of the numerous rock shelters lining the canyon walls of the southern mesa. This provided not only the rock-sheltered building locations, but also a source of drinking water for those who would later settle here.

The Anasazi (Navajo word for "ancient ones") were the inhabitants of Mesa Verde. Their culture developed here over a span of 1,300 years. Their advances and lifestyle changes are grouped into four main periods. The first, Basketmaker I and II, began about 2,000 years ago and lasted to around A.D. 500. During this time, the Anasazi lived in the canyon's rock shelters and mastered the art of weaving baskets, which were used both for storing and cooking. Tools and ornaments were also manufactured. They grew corn and squash on the mesa top and in the canyons, storing this produce in their caves for winter consumption. Their diet was supplemented with game, which they hunted with an arrow-throwing stick called the atlatl.

Advances were made between A.D. 500 and 750 during the Basketmaker III period. The Anasazi moved to the mesa tops where they used mud and pole techniques to construct pithouses. They also learned to produce pottery. Beans were added as a cultivated crop, and they domesticated and raised turkeys, a source of food and decorative feathers. The bow and arrow

STATE OF COLORADO

Cliff Palace is one of the largest dwellings in the park.

U.S. DEPARTMENT OF INTERIOR, NATIONAL PARK SERVICE

Spruce Tree House is open for year-round visitation.

19 MESA VERDE NATIONAL PARK

came into use, replacing the less effective atlatl. Pithouses were eventually built in small groups, or villages.

Progress marked Pueblo I and Pueblo II periods, from A.D. 750 to 1100. Houses, now constructed with a variety of building materials, continued to be placed in groups, often centered around a circular ceremonial building called the kiva. A new level of quality was evident in their pottery, and cotton, probably acquired through trade, was used to weave cloth.

Most of the Anasazi remains we see today at Mesa Verde are from the Pueblo III period, which lasted from A.D. 1100 to 1300. Building skills reached a peak with the fine masonry multistory cliff dwellings that line the canyon walls. The influence of religion continued to grow, as is evidenced by the many ceremonial kivas among the pueblo complexes. The craftsmanship reflected in their elaborately decorated pottery also reached its zenith. They continued to manufacture quality cloth, tools, and ornaments. Eventually, the mesa tops were stripped of firewood, and the once rich agricultural soil became depleted. A 24-year drought starting in 1276 probably induced the abandonment of Mesa Verde during the late 1200s.

Pioneer photographer William Henry Jackson, attached to the Hayden Survey, was the first to photograph a few of the ruins in 1874. In 1888 Richard Wetherill and Charles Mason, local ranchers, were the first to see the remains of Cliff Palace. Frederick Chapin, who was led to the ruins by members of the Wetherill family, published the first account of the ruins in 1892. In 1893 an archaeological report was published by Baron Gustav Nordenskiold of Sweden, who conducted the first excavation of the ruins in 1891. He too was guided by the Wetherills. The ruins were commercially exploited through the 1890s and early 1900s, and Mesa Verde antiquities were sold to any interested buyers. In 1906 Mesa Verde National Park was established to protect it against further commercialization. Since that time, the ruins have been properly excavated and stabilized.

Today the Ruins Road leads to a variety of ruins on Chapin Mesa, including mesa-top structures and cliff dwellings. Some ruins tours are ranger-conducted and others self-guided. The Ruins Road closes at sunset. Hiking is restricted to established trails within the park; you should register before taking any of the longer hikes. Ruins on Wetherill Mesa can be reached only by a shuttle bus which runs daily during the summer season. Even though the Ruins Road is kept open all year, Cliff Palace and Balcony House cliff dwellings are closed from mid-November to mid-April by snow. Tours of Spruce Tree House are conducted all year, weather permitting. There are numerous services available in the park during the summer season.

DIRECTIONS: From the junction <0.0> of US 666 and US 160 at the west end of Cortez, proceed east on US 160 to the well-marked entrance road< 10.4> to Mesa Verde National Park. The road heads south and climbs to the mesa top on its way to the visitor center (15 miles) and southern ruins areas (21 miles). Allow 45 minutes for the entrance road drive.

MESA VERDE NATIONAL PARK

Courtesy of USDA Forest Service

TELLURIDE DISTRICT

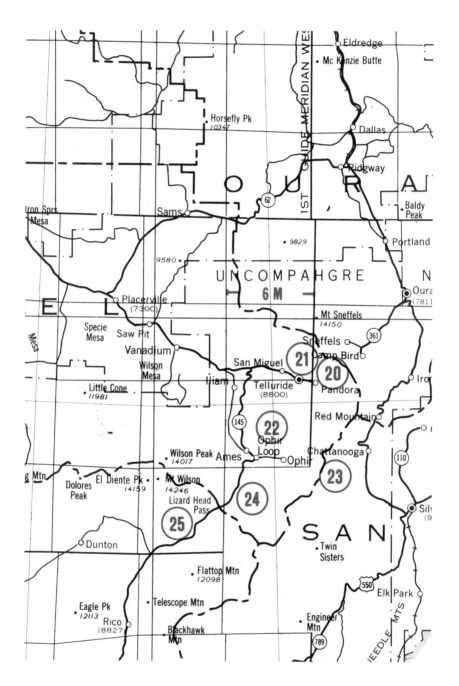

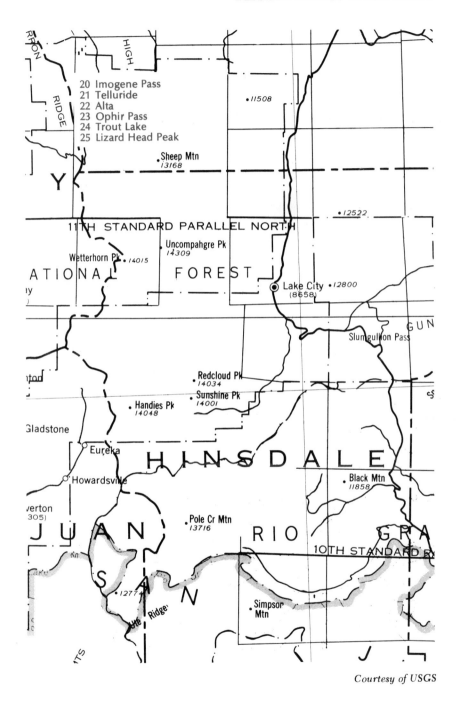

20 Imogene Pass
21 Telluride
22 Alta
23 Ophir Pass
24 Trout Lake
25 Lizard Head Peak

• 11508

• Sheep Mtn
13168

11TH STANDARD PARALLEL NORTH

• 12522

Uncompahgre Pk
14309

Wetterhorn Pk • 14015

ATIONAL   FOREST

⊙ Lake City • 12800
(8658)

GUN

Slumgullion Pass

• Redcloud Pk
14034

• Sunshine Pk
14001

• Handies Pk
14048

Gladstone

○ Eureka

HINSDALE

○ Howardsville

• Black Mtn
11858

verton
305)

JUAN

• Pole Cr Mtn
13716

RIO   GRA

10TH STANDARD R

SAN

• 12771

Ute Ridge

Simpson
Mtn

TS

J

Courtesy of USGS

20   IMOGENE PASS

                 TYPE: Mountain Scenery/Historic
       ADMINISTRATION: Private land/Uncompahgre National Forest
             QUALITY: Superbly scenic
              ACCESS: Difficult 4WD
          FACILITIES: None
        TIME NEEDED: Four hours
          BEST VISIT: Midsummer to late summer
         BEST PHOTO: All day
           ELEVATION: 13,114 feet
           REFERENCE: Telluride
                  MAP: Uncompahgre National Forest visitor map
           USGS TOPO: Ironton 7.5' (1972)
                         Telluride 7.5' (1955)
       USGS COUNTY: San Miguel County Sheet 3 of 3 (1978)
                         Ouray County Sheet 2 of 2 (1975)

Imogene Pass is one of the highest and toughest passes in Colorado. For about two months a year (mid-July to mid-September), a difficult four-wheel-drive road is passable between Telluride and Ouray over Imogene Pass. Views of the San Juan Mountains from along this road are among the best in Colorado. Even though four-wheel-drive vehicles can be rented in both Telluride and Ouray, this road is not for beginners. If you are not an experienced jeeper, try a conducted tour over Imogene Pass which departs from Ouray. It is also possible for drivers of passenger cars to enjoy some of this scenery by following Colorado 361 from Ouray toward Camp Bird Mine and Yankee Boy Basin.

There is a famous mine located on each side of the pass: Tomboy on the Telluride side and Camp Bird on the Ouray side. In the 1870s an early use of the pass was to carry Tomboy ore by pack mule to Ouray. As the network of tunnels grew beneath the pass from both mines, the road saw heavier use, but with the decline of mining in the 1920s, the road fell into disrepair. Only ruins remain of the Tomboy, but the Camp Bird, a consistent producer, is still in good condition.

During the early 1900s the local mines were undergoing labor disputes. Trouble began in 1902, culminating in a long strike in 1903. After shots were exchanged at the Smuggler-Union Mine in Telluride, victorious union members forced non-union workers to march over Imogene Pass and warned them to keep going. The mine owners asked Colorado Governor James Peabody to send in the National Guard, and troop trains arrived carrying 500 men. Telluride was declared under martial law as the state militia surrounded the town. Union members were deported by train. There was even a small fort, Fort Peabody, built above Imogene Pass to prevent union reinforcements from sneaking into Telluride. This fort was manned by troops through the winter of 1903-04. Few places are less hospitable than Imogene Pass in the winter.

The Imogene Pass Road offers good views of Telluride.

The road passes along the edge of a high cliff directly above the Camp Bird Mine.

20 IMOGENE PASS

DIRECTIONS: On the main east-west street (Colorado Avenue) in downtown Telluride, go one block west of the San Miguel County Courthouse, turn right, go one block north, turn right, go one block east, turn left onto North Oak Street, and follow it north to a stop sign <0.0>.

Turn right onto the Imogene Pass Road, marked by a small sign as Forest Route 869. Follow the road as it starts to climb out of Telluride. Stay on the main road; ignore a switchback <1.2> to the left. There are a few spots along the road that offer a bird's eye view of Telluride below. There are also good views <1.8> toward the east end of the Telluride Valley, containing Ingram Falls on the left, the Black Bear Pass Road switchbacks in the center, and Bridal Veil Falls on the right. Eventually, this narrow shelf road reaches the high Savage Basin, containing the remains of the huge Tomboy Mine. It is usually possible for two-wheel-drive pick-up trucks to reach the Tomboy Mine <4.7>.

Above the Tomboy Mine, the road becomes a difficult four-wheel-drive road <5.3>. There are also numerous side roads crisscrossing the mining area. Try to stay on the main road as it winds through the floor of the basin toward the east. At the east wall of the basin, the road switchbacks up to a shelf road that heads north toward Imogene Pass, the low, colorful ridge forming the northeast rim of the basin. A small register box marks the summit <6.9> of the pass. Views from the pass and from the ridge that runs southeast from the pass toward Telluride Peak (13,509 feet) are beyond description.

Just beyond the pass, the road descends steeply into Imogene Basin. Again, there is a maze of jeep roads, most of which rejoin the main road. Stay on what appears to be the main route. Keep right where a side road <9.1> on the left goes to the Upper Camp Bird Mine. Cross a feeble-looking bridge <9.8> and then ford the creek <10.1>. Keep left and climb the hill at a fork <10.8> marked by a beat-up sign with a left arrow indicating Ouray and Yankee Boy Basin. The road climbs and then levels off along the rim of a high cliff with an impressive, but chilling, view <11.0> of the Camp Bird Mine below. The road continues through a muddy bog with a good rock bottom, fords a stream, and joins with a good dirt road <12.2> (Colorado 361) leading to Ouray. You may wish to turn left to explore Yankee Boy Basin.

To reach Ouray, turn right at this junction and continue over an exciting, but safe, shelf road that descends to the entrance <13.5> of the Camp Bird Mine. Continue straight on the main road to reach a paved section <15.2> of Colorado 361. The pavement comes and goes, and the road passes the entrance <17.9> to Box Canyon Falls (see site 28) just before reaching US 550 <18.0>. Turn left for Ouray.

Passenger cars can follow Colorado 361 up from Ouray to the junction with the Imogene Pass Road and a little beyond toward Yankee Boy Basin. Two-wheel-drive vehicles coming from Ouray should not turn left onto the Imogene Pass Road or continue all the way to Yankee Boy Basin, since the last few miles become too rough.

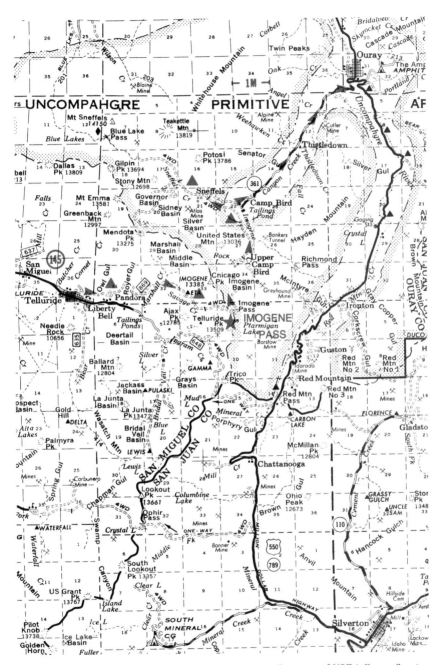

Courtesy of USDA Forest Service

21 TELLURIDE

TYPE: Mountain Scenery/Historic
ADMINISTRATION: Private land
QUALITY: Extremely scenic
ACCESS: Paved road
FACILITIES: Commercial attractions
TIME NEEDED: One hour
BEST VISIT: Spring to fall
BEST PHOTO: Afternoon
ELEVATION: 8,745 feet
REFERENCE: Telluride
MAP: State highway map
Uncompahgre National Forest visitor map
USGS TOPO: Telluride 7.5' (1955)
USGS COUNTY: San Miguel County Sheet 3 of 3 (1978)

Telluride is named for the element tellurium, which is often associated with gold and silver ores found in this mining district. During the town's boom days, it was also referred to as "To-hell-you-ride." Over $350,000,000 in precious ores have been extracted from the valley, and several mines are still active.

In 1875 John Fallon staked the Ajax, Ausboro, Emerald, and Sheridan claims along the valley. His partner staked adjoining claims but lost rights of ownership because he failed to invest $100 in improvements to each claim as required by Colorado mining law. The famous Smuggler-Union mine was later struck on one of these forfeited claims. The Smuggler-Union vein assayed at $1,200 per ton and started a rush to Telluride. Rich strikes continued into the 1880s. Some of the best producers were the Liberty Bell, Tomboy, Black Bear, Cimarron, Japan, Columbia, Bullion, Red Cloud, Hidden Treasure, Champion, Argentine, Snow Drift, Andrews, and Cleveland. By one estimate there are over 275 miles of tunnels deep into the surrounding canyon walls.

All this prosperity did not escape the opportune notice of the McCarty Gang which included George LeRoy Parker, otherwise known as Butch Cassidy. Butch had previously worked in Telluride and knew the town well. The gang picked the San Miguel Valley Bank, known to handle large mine payrolls, as their target. On the morning of June 24, 1889, only the book-keeper was left in the bank. Butch Cassidy, Tom McCarty, and Matt Warner entered and helped themselves to all the cash in sight, just over $10,000. They backed out of the bank, mounted their horses being held by Bert Maddern and quickly left Telluride. After the alarm was spread, Sheriff Wasson and a posse took out after the gang. The posse had no chance of catching them, since the gang had wisely stationed fresh horses at pre-planned intervals. The gang headed south toward Mancos and then through eastern Utah to Brown's Park, a notorious bandit hideout in northwestern

At the east end of the Telluride Valley, the remains of a power station stand beside Bridal Veil Falls.

21 TELLURIDE

Colorado. This early event in Cassidy's career helped to establish his fame as one of the West's most colorful outlaws.

Real prosperity came when the town's two major problems were solved: power and transportation. After the Ames power station (see site 24) was completed in 1890, an extension high-voltage line was run to the Telluride Valley. Electric motors were then used to replace steam power at the mines and mills. Thus, the world's first long-distance alternating-current power system supplied inexpensive power that made the difference between profitability and failure of many mines.

Prior to 1890 all merchandise and ore had to be freighted between Telluride and Ouray. Freighting was expensive. Otto Mears not only built miraculous wagon roads through the San Juan Mountains but was determined to link the Telluride mining district with Silverton and Ouray by rail. He started construction of the narrow-gauge Rio Grande Southern Railroad in 1890, financed with over $5,000,000. Work began at Durango and Ridgway, and both routes headed toward Telluride. The 46-mile Ridgway section, which followed the route of Mears's toll road over Dallas Divide (see site 27), was completed to Telluride on November 15, 1890. Construction continued south from Telluride toward Rico to meet the advancing rails from Durango. The amazing Ophir Loop was engineered to raise the grade from the San Miguel Valley to the level of Trout Lake (see site 24). The route continued over Lizard Head Pass (see site 25), the high point on the line at 10,250 feet. The rails were joined eleven miles south of Rico in December, 1891.

Inexpensive shipping rates brought by the railroad spurred new activity in the Telluride Valley, but only until the silver panic of 1893. Previous changes in federal policy concerning the purchase of gold versus silver as a monetary standard eventually led to a depressed silver price. After the value of silver dropped more than half, many mines closed, and the Rio Grande Southern went bankrupt. Despite its financial losses, the railroad found ways to keep running until 1951. The Galloping Goose, a splice between a box car and a Pierce Arrow automobile, was used as a cost effective means to shuttle a few passengers and 10,000 pounds of freight between Durango and Ridgway. Several of these contraptions were built, and one is now on display in Telluride. The railroad also carried the uranium ore used in the World War II atomic bomb project (see site 7).

Telluride, located in a box canyon, is one of Colorado's most scenic towns. The east end of the valley is spectacular. The incredible switchbacks of the Black Bear Road, one of Colorado's most hazardous jeep roads, boldly climb the east wall of the valley. South of the road is the beautiful Bridal Veil Falls which drops 365 feet from a small power station perched on the rim of the canyon. North of the road is Ingram Falls. Telluride has a ski area, a worthwhile museum (317 North First Street), and many other attractions for the visitor. Four-wheel-drive vehicles can be rented and tours can be arranged to explore the surrounding backcountry.

DIRECTIONS: Telluride is at the end of Colorado 145 Spur which heads four miles east from Colorado 145 between Placerville and Rico.

You may wish to continue east through Telluride to the end of the valley. From there, you can enjoy views of Bridal Veil Falls (on the south wall) and Ingram Falls (on the north wall). Travel on the hazardous Black Bear Road, which climbs the east valley wall with narrow switchbacks, is not recommended. However, you may wish to hike this road to reach to the top of Bridal Veil Falls which offers a beautiful view of the valley below.

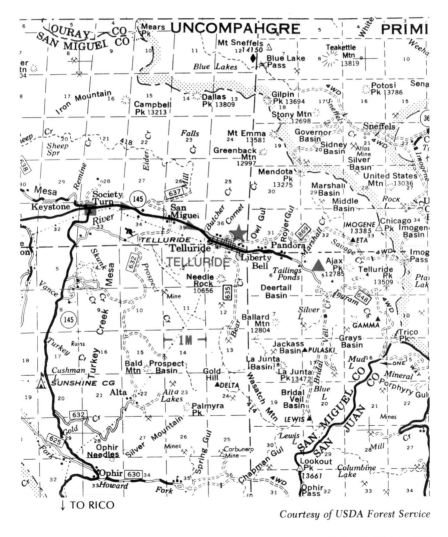

Courtesy of USDA Forest Service

22 ALTA

TYPE: Mountain Scenery/Historic
ADMINISTRATION: Private land
QUALITY: Very scenic
ACCESS: Dirt road
FACILITIES: Nearby campground
TIME NEEDED: One hour
BEST VISIT: Early summer to fall
BEST PHOTO: Afternoon
ELEVATION: 11,045 feet
REFERENCE: Telluride
MAP: Uncompahgre National Forest visitor map
USGS TOPO: Telluride 7.5' (1955)
USGS COUNTY: San Miguel County Sheet 3 of 3 (1978)

Alta, once rich in minerals, is also rich in scenery. The few buildings of Alta, still in reasonable condition, stand against a background of the Ophir Needles, Lizard Head Peak (see site 25), and three "fourteeners": Mount Wilson, Wilson Peak, and El Diente Peak. Alta Lakes, just east of town, form reflecting pools for this same scenery.

Mineral discoveries in 1877 led to the development of the Gold King Mine. This single mine, just south of town, was the basic support for Alta through the 1890s. The ore yielded both gold and silver as well as copper and lead. The Four Metals Company of Milwaukee purchased the site in 1904 and worked it sporadically for the next 13 years. The property was operated by John Wagner for the Belmont and Tonopah Mining Company until 1924. Beginning in 1938, after an inactive period, the site was managed by H.F. Klock unitl 1945. Alta is now the property of the Silver Mountain Mining Company which does allow sightseers to visit the site, provided that they do not enter the buildings or deface or remove any of the property.

Alta still contains a few cabins, houses, mining buildings, and a large boardinghouse. The camp never had a church, and the three mills at Alta have since burned. The Saint Louis and Alta veins, reached by the nearly two-mile long Black Hawk tunnel, have yielded nearly $20,000,000 in precious metals.

DIRECTIONS: From the junction <0.0> of Colorado 145 and Colorado 145 Spur at Telluride, proceed south on Colorado 145 past Sunshine Campground to a side road <5.4> on the left, marked by a sign identifying access to Alta Lakes (4 miles). Turn left and follow this dirt road. The first portion of the road is narrow with few places to pass, but is no real hazard to passenger cars. Continue past a good view <7.1> of the Ophir Needles (to the east) to the main part of Alta <9.2>. Here a sign reminds you that this is private property and to please not enter or deface the buildings. Vehicles should return the way they came and not continue on the Boomerang Road to Telluride.

KEN JESSEN

This old boardinghouse once provided shelter for the workers of the Gold King Mine.

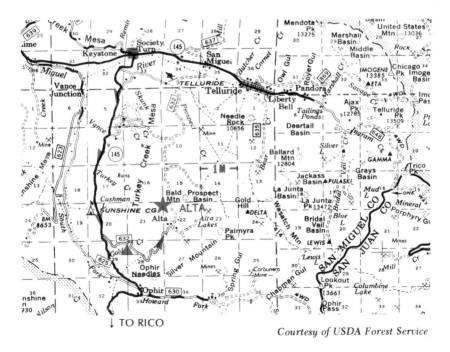

↓ TO RICO

Courtesy of USDA Forest Service

23 OPHIR PASS

TYPE: Mountain Scenery/Historic
ADMINISTRATION: Uncompahgre and San Juan National Forests
QUALITY: Extremely scenic
ACCESS: Easy 4WD
FACILITIES: None
TIME NEEDED: Two hours
BEST VISIT: Midsummer to late summer
BEST PHOTO: Afternoon
ELEVATION: 11,750 feet
REFERENCE: Silverton
MAP: Uncompahgre National Forest visitor map
USGS TOPO: Ophir 7.5' (1955)
USGS COUNTY: San Miguel County Sheet 3 of 3 (1978)
San Juan County (1975)

Ophir, the Biblical location of King Solomon's mines, lends its name to an old town, a new town, and a spectacular San Juan mountain pass. Old Ophir was established in the 1870s as a silver camp. Its population peaked at about 500. New Ophir was settled later and was a stop on the Rio Grande Southern Railroad at the legendary Ophir Loop. The pass was first used in the 1870s as mineral exploration opened the region. A toll road was built across Ophir Pass in 1881 and became a major route connecting Silverton with Telluride. The pass road is still heavily used for its scenic value.

The view from the pass is spectacular. To the east are the iron-stained peaks near Red Mountain Pass. To the west, Old Ophir and New Ophir are contained in the valley of the Howard Fork of the San Miguel River. Beyond the mouth of this valley is a ridge of lofty "fourteeners": Mount Wilson, Wilson Peak, and El Diente Peak. The shelf road descending the west side of the pass is cut across the vividly colored slide rock that fills the northeastern rim of the valley. The bright hues of yellow, orange, and red result from iron oxides in the rock.

The directions for Ophir Pass start from the Silverton side because the route is a one-way road from the pass to Old Ophir. This easy four-wheel-drive road is a good choice for beginners. Four-wheel-drive vehicles can be rented in Silverton, Ouray, and Telluride. Conducted tours over Ophir Pass depart from Ouray. If you are in a passenger car, it is worth the trip from Colorado 145 to Old Ophir to view this colorful pass.

DIRECTIONS: From Silverton <0.0> proceed north on US 550 to a marked side road <4.9> on the left. Turn left and follow this easy jeep road as it descends to a one-lane bridge <5.2>, keeps right at a switchback <8.0>, and then climbs to Ophir Pass <9.3>. Continue down on the one-way shelf road to Old Ophir <12.8> and then to New Ophir at Colorado 145 <14.9>.

LEE GREGORY

The Ophir Pass Road is cut along this colorful slide rock of the northeastern valley rim.

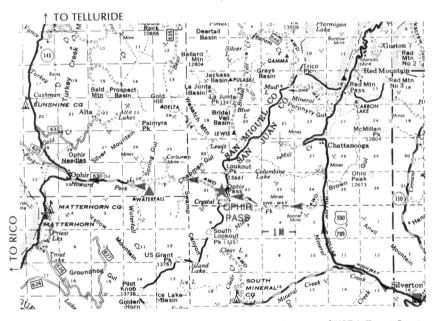

Courtesy of USDA Forest Service

24 TROUT LAKE

TYPE: Mountain Scenery
ADMINISTRATION: Private land
QUALITY: Very scenic
ACCESS: Paved road
FACILITIES: Nearby campgrounds and Rest rooms
TIME NEEDED: Half hour
BEST VISIT: Spring to fall
BEST PHOTO: Afternoon
ELEVATION: 9,710 feet
REFERENCE: Telluride
MAP: State highway map
Uncompahgre National Forest visitor map
USGS TOPO: Mount Wilson 7.5' (1953)
USGS COUNTY: San Miguel County Sheet 3 of 3 (1978)

Trout Lake is one of Colorado's most scenic lakes. At the foot of Lizard Head Pass, the lake is set against a background of high and colorful peaks. To the north is Yellow Mountain (12,713 feet), to the south is Sheep Mountain (13,188 feet), and to the west is Vermilion Peak (13,894 feet). The Rio Grande Southern Railroad once made a loop around the west end of the lake to lose elevation from Lizard Head Pass. A water tower still stands at the lake.

Trout Lake is the reservoir for one of the most historic power plants in the world. Water leaves the lake through the Illium Flume and is piped down a vertical cliff to a small hydroelectric generating station at Ames in the valley below. This was the first commercial alternating-current generation station in the world, and it is still operating today.

In the 1880s a kind of technical war was underway. Up to that time, all electrical systems had been of the direct-current variety, invented by Thomas Edison. However, DC power systems have the disadvantage of being inefficient when distributed over long distances. Nikola Tesla, inventor of the alternating-current system, advocated AC as a solution to the distribution problem. However, an AC system had never been commercially demonstrated, and experts like Edison thought it could never succeed.

Lucien Nunn, manager of the Gold King Mine in Alta (see site 22), searched for a cheaper way to operate his machinery, which was costing $2,500 per month in steam power. He enlisted the aid of George Westinghouse to implement the ideas of Tesla. The Ames plant was built, and in 1890 a three-mile long, 3,000-volt power line supplied the Gold King Mine, reducing its power cost to $500 a month. Later, lines were run long distances to power surrounding mines. With this success, the Westinghouse Company triumphed over the Edison Electric Company and set the modern standard.

DIRECTIONS: Trout Lake is located just east of Colorado 145, 1.6 miles north of Lizard Head Pass and 10.4 miles south of Colorado 145 Spur.

STATE OF COLORADO

Yellow Mountain, Vermilion Peak, and Sheep Mountain form the background of Trout Lake.

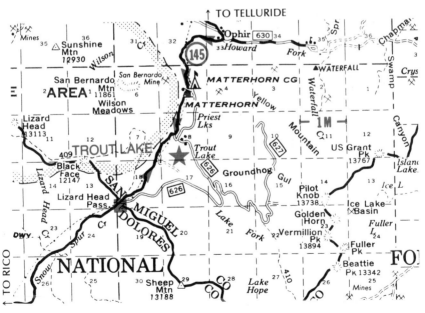

Also see map on page 97.

Courtesy of USDA Forest Service

25 LIZARD HEAD PEAK

TYPE: Mountain Scenery
ADMINISTRATION: San Juan National Forest
QUALITY: Scenic
ACCESS: Paved road
FACILITIES: Rest rooms at Lizard Head Pass
TIME NEEDED: Quarter hour
BEST VISIT: Spring to fall
BEST PHOTO: Morning to midday
ELEVATION: 13,113 feet
REFERENCE: Telluride
MAP: State highway map
San Juan National Forest visitor map
USGS TOPO: Mount Wilson 7.5' (1953)
USGS COUNTY: Dolores County Sheet 3 of 3 (1976)

Lizard Head is a dramatic spire protruding from a ridge of mountains known as the San Miguel Range. Rising more than 400 feet above the top of an already lofty mountain, the vertical, sheer-walled monolith is a product of the region's volcanic past. Before a large piece fell off, the spire more closely resembled the head of a lizard. West of Lizard Head are three spectacular "fourteeners": Wilson Peak (14,017 feet), Mount Wilson (14,246 feet), and El Diente Peak (14,159 feet). Lizard Head Wilderness now encompasses much of this scenery.

Many feel that Lizard Head is the toughest technical climb in Colorado. It was declared "absolutely insurmountable" in a 1932 United States Geologic Survey report. The report was not entirely accurate, since Lizard Head had already been scaled in 1920. Albert Ellingwood and his climbing partner, Barton Hoag, hiked from Lizard Head Pass to the base of the pillar with their early climbing equipment. They reported that it was a rotten mass of rock, that a hand could dislodge hundreds of pounds of rubble, and that spontaneous avalanches could be heard all around. The ascent was perilous, and at one point the lead climber had to stand on his partner's shoulders to find a hand-hold. The pair conquered the summit and returned safely.

Lizard Head Pass (10,222 feet), just east of the peak, had for years been crossed by a well-worn trail when a wagon road was built in the 1870s. It was also the high point on the Rio Grande Southern Railroad which has an incredible history. There was also a short-lived mining camp at the pass during the San Juan mining boom.

DIRECTIONS: Lizard Head Peak can be seen to the northwest from a large turnout on the west side of Colorado 145. This turnout is 2.0 miles south of Lizard Head Pass and is marked by a sign (readable only if you are northbound on Colorado 145). Lizard Head Pass is on Colorado 145, 12.2 miles north of Rico and 12.0 miles south of the junction of Colorado 145 and Colorado 145 Spur at Telluride.

LEE GREGORY

The isolated spire of Lizard Head Peak rises 400 feet above an already lofty mountain.

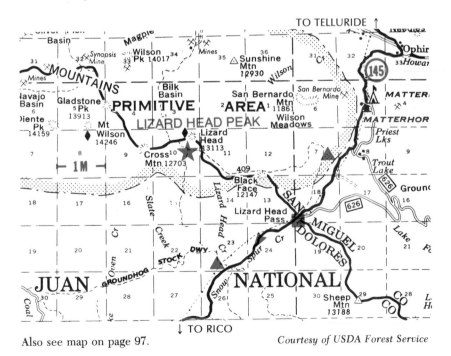

Also see map on page 97.

Courtesy of USDA Forest Service

SAN JUAN DISTRICT

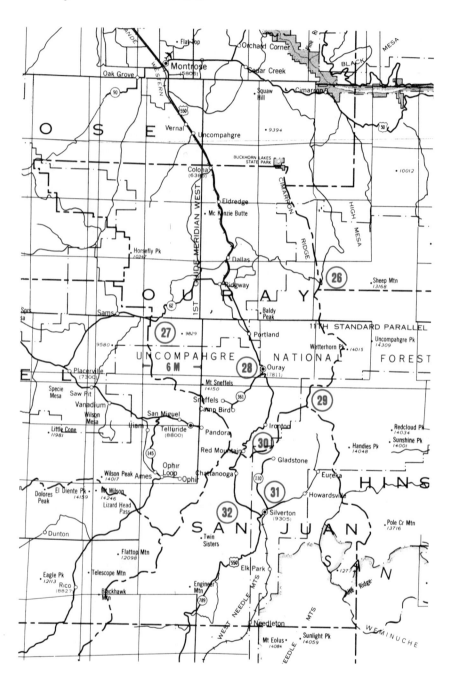

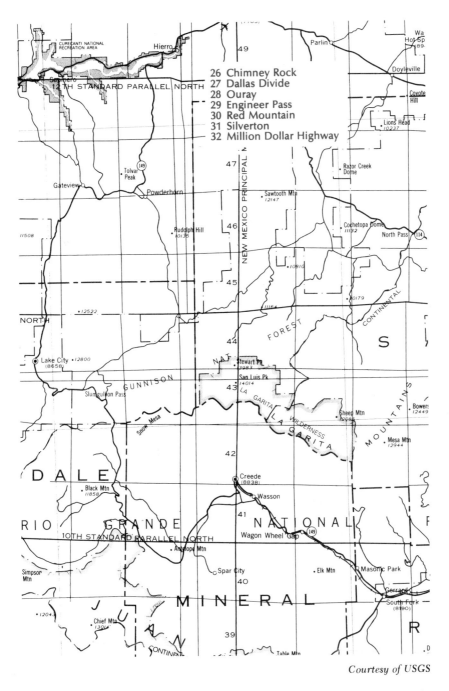

26 Chimney Rock
27 Dallas Divide
28 Ouray
29 Engineer Pass
30 Red Mountain
31 Silverton
32 Million Dollar Highway

Courtesy of USGS

26 CHIMNEY ROCK

TYPE: Mountain Scenery/Geologic
ADMINISTRATION: Uncompahgre National Forest
QUALITY: Very scenic
ACCESS: Good dirt road
FACILITIES: Campgrounds/Picnic areas
TIME NEEDED: Two hours
BEST VISIT: Early summer to fall
BEST PHOTO: Afternoon
ELEVATION: 11,781 feet
REFERENCE: Ridgway
MAP: Uncompahgre National Forest visitor map
USGS TOPO: Courthouse Mountain 7.5′ (1963)
USGS COUNTY: Gunnison County Sheet 6 of 6 (1975)
Hinsdale County Sheet 1 of 2 (1978)
Ouray County Sheet 1 of 2 (1975)

Chimney Rock and Courthouse Mountain (12,040 feet) form part of Cimarron Ridge which separates the Cimarron and Uncompahgre river basins. A long, but scenic, dirt road traverses this region, connecting Ridgway and Cimarron. The road passes locations used in the 1969 western *True Grit* and crosses Cimarron Ridge at Owl Creek Pass (10,114 feet), just north of Chimney Rock and Courthouse Mountain. The road then descends into the valley of the Cimarron River with spectacular views into the San Juan Mountains to the south. Farther north Silver Jack Overlook provides rest rooms, picnic areas, and a fine view. If road conditions permit, you may wish to explore the scenery along the side roads that continue up the West and Middle forks of the Cimarron River.

The jagged and sculpted scenery in this region results from a different geologic structure than is found elsewhere in the San Juans. The local terrain is composed of San Juan tuff, volcanic ash that has been compressed into rock. This tuff has weathered into the blockish Courthouse Mountain and the intricate palisades along the eastern side of the Cimarron River.

DIRECTIONS: From the junction <0.0> of US 550 and Colorado 62 in Ridgway, proceed north on US 550. Turn right onto a good dirt road <1.9> marked by a sign indicating national forest access for Owl Creek Pass (13 miles) and Silver Jack Reservoir (20 miles). You are now on Ouray County 10, which passes through 9 miles of private property. Keep left at a sign <2.8> directing you toward Uncompahgre National Forest. Go straight at another sign <4.6> indicating Owl Creek Pass and Cow Creek. Keep right at a sign <6.0> directing you toward Uncompahgre National Forest. Cross a bridge <7.0> and turn left at a junction <7.4> marked by a sign directing you to Uncompahgre National Forest. Keep left as you go uphill at a sign <7.7> identifying Owl Creek Road. Keep left where a side road <11.8> on the right goes to Spaulding Park. Again, keep left where a side road <13.0>

LEE GREGORY

Majestic Chimney Rock rises above ragged Courthouse Mountain.

on the right goes to Flume Creek. Pass good views <13.1> of Chimney Rock and keep right at a side road <14.4> on the left leading to Nate Creek.

There is a good view across the meadow <16.4> where the shootout scene in the movie *True Grit* was filmed. A sign at the west end of this meadow points to Chimney Rock. Cross Owl Creek Pass <17.0> to reach a junction <17.3> with a side road to the right identified by a sign as access to the West Fork of the Cimarron River. Continue on the main road where a sign <18.7> identifies Turret Ridge. Continue over a bridge <20.0>, go straight at a side road <23.5> on the left, and cross another bridge to reach a side road <23.7> on the right, marked by a sign as access to the Middle Fork of the Cimarron River. Continuing on the main road, cross a bridge to reach a T-intersection <23.8>.

Directly east from this junction is a fine example of the palisades of the Cimarron River. A sign indicates a left turn for the Jackson Ranger Station and a right turn for the East Fork of the Cimarron River. The side road to the right is usually too rough for passenger cars.

Turn left and continue on the main road past the Jackson Ranger Station <24.5> to reach the Silver Jack Reservoir Overlook <26.2> on the left. Continue on the main road past Silver Jack Campground <26.6>, Beaver Lake Campground <27.9>, and Big Cimarron Campground <28.6> to reach the Uncompahgre National Forest boundary <28.7>. Continue on the main road, keeping right where a side road <37.6> labeled P77 joins from the left, to reach US 50 <43.6>. Turn left for Montrose.

LEE GREGORY

Palisades of volcanic tuff line the eastern wall of the Cimarron River Valley.

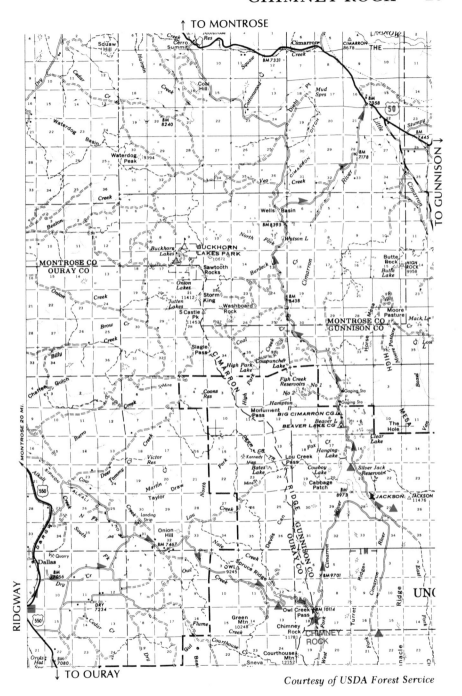

Courtesy of USDA Forest Service

27 DALLAS DIVIDE

TYPE:	Mountain Scenery
ADMINISTRATION:	Private land
QUALITY:	Very scenic
ACCESS:	Paved road
FACILITIES:	None
TIME NEEDED:	Half hour
BEST VISIT:	Spring to fall
BEST PHOTO:	Afternoon to late afternoon
ELEVATION:	8,970 feet
REFERENCE:	Ridgway
MAP:	State highway map
	Uncompahgre National Forest visitor map
USGS TOPO:	Sams 7.5' (1967)
USGS COUNTY:	Ouray County Sheet 2 of 2 (1975)
	San Miguel County Sheet 3 of 3 (1978)

Dallas Divide offers an incredible view of the Sneffels Range, one of the most rugged and spectacular regions of the San Juan Mountains. Mount Sneffels, highest point on the skyline to the south, is one of Colorado's "fourteeners" at a height of 14,150 feet. Other jagged peaks along this mountain wall average about 13,500 feet.

Dallas Divide is the high point of Colorado 62, connecting Ridgway and Placerville. This road originally started as another of Otto Mears's numerous toll roads. In fact, 13,496-foot Mears Peak, almost directly south of Dallas Divide, is named in his honor. Opened in 1882, the road was little more than muddy ruts, and it didn't improve with use. Despite this rough route, much freight was hauled into Telluride during its mining boom.

Mears didn't stop there, however. Dallas Divide was also the route used by his narrow gauge railroad, the Rio Grande Southern. The first train made it from Durango to Ridgway on December 21, 1891. This venture never turned a profit, but it is one of the most interesting chapters in the history of Colorado railroading.

One of the first automobiles to cross Dallas Divide made the trip in a mere 15 hours during the 1900s. Today, the paved highway makes for a quick trip from Ridgway to Placerville. In contrast, the scenery has changed little and can't be improved. Please enjoy the view from the highway, since Dallas Divide is mostly surrounded by private land.

DIRECTIONS: From the junction <0.0> of US 550 and Colorado 62 in Ridgway, follow Colorado 62 west to a small turnout <10.2> on the left side of the road, marked by a blue "scenic overlook" sign. From here, the view to the south is spectacular. The highway continues over Dallas Divide <10.7> to join Colorado 145 <23.2> at Placerville.

LEE GREGORY

Dallas Divide offers a fine view of the beautiful Sneffels Range.

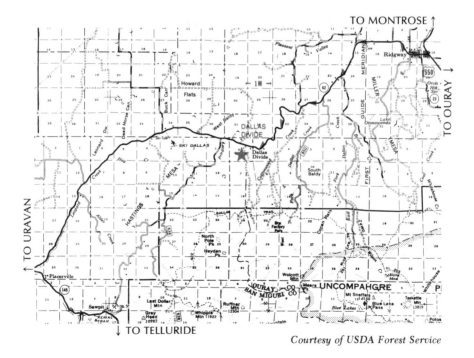

Courtesy of USDA Forest Service

28 OURAY

TYPE: Mountain Scenery/Historic
ADMINISTRATION: Private land
QUALITY: Very scenic
ACCESS: Paved road
FACILITIES: Commercial attractions
TIME NEEDED: Two hours
BEST VISIT: Spring to fall
BEST PHOTO: Midday to afternoon
ELEVATION: 7,706 feet
REFERENCE: Ouray
MAP: State highway map
Uncompahgre National Forest visitor map
USGS TOPO: Ouray 7.5' (1955)
USGS COUNTY: Ouray County Sheet 2 of 2 (1975)

Ouray, named for the Ute Indian chief, marks the northern bounds of the "Switzerland of America." Some of the nation's most spectacular mountain scenery extends south from Ouray along the Million Dollar Highway (see site 32). But it was not the scenery that brought the first settlers to Ouray.

In 1875 Gus Begole and Jack Eckles came north from Silverton (see site 31) in search of gold and silver. They found it. One of the early rich strikes was made by Logan Whitlock and A. J. Staley, two sportsmen who stumbled across a promising site while seaching for a good fishing hole. By 1876 Ouray was an incorporated town and soon had the normal assortment of mining businesses: stores, saloons, hotels, gambling houses, smelters, and several newspapers. Ouray's most notorious paper was the *Solid Muldoon* which printed the irreverent opinions of its unpredictable publisher, David Frakes Day. Distributed from 1879 to 1892, the *Solid Muldoon* was probably Colorado's most colorful newspaper.

Ouray thrived on silver mining until the panic of 1893 when the Sherman Silver Purchase Act was repealed. The town then entered a recession that lasted for three years. In 1895 Thomas Walsh, operator of a small smelter in Silverton, paid an assistant to recover samples from abandoned mines along Canyon Creek, west of Ouray. Walsh discovered that this waste rock contained a high concentration of a gold-telluride ore (see site 21) that had been totally ignored by earlier prospectors. This find became the fabulous Camp Bird Mine. This immense gold discovery started a second boom, and the town prospered past the turn of the century. Walsh moved his family to Ouray and used part of his $9,000,000 in mining proceeds to purchase the Hope Diamond, the world's most famous gem, for his wife.

Today Ouray's beautiful setting in a natural amphitheater attracts many visitors. The town offers many services for the vacationer, including four-wheel-drive rentals and a fine audio-visual program. Regularly scheduled tours leave Ouray in multipassenger four-wheel-drive vehicles to reach some of the most spectacular mountain scenery in the nation. The Ouray

LEE GREGORY

Box Canyon Falls is nearly enclosed in rock.

County Historical Museum (Sixth Avenue and Third Street) is worth a visit.

At the western edge of town is Box Canyon Park, administered by the city. The park encompasses Box Canyon of Canyon Creek. This 20-foot wide, 285-foot deep canyon has been cut by stream erosion along a geologic fault through a relatively soft limestone layer. Inside this cleft is Box Canyon Falls which drops 227 feet and is almost surrounded by solid rock. In this confined space the roar of the falling water is deafening, and its spray coats the interior walls. Sightseers were first able to view the falls in the late 1890s after the local power company blasted part of the canyon's entrance for a water line. The present park has two short trails. The lower trail enters Box Canyon and follows a series of wooden walks to the falls. The steep upper trail leads to High Bridge, directly above Canyon Creek where it dives into the rock to form the falls. There is also a good view of Ouray to the east from the bridge. The park collects a small fee.

DIRECTIONS: Ouray is located on US 550, 37 miles south of Montrose and 23 miles north of Silverton. To reach Box Canyon Falls follow US 550 south just outside of town. Turn right onto a side road (Colorado 361) marked as national forest access to Camp Bird Mine and Yankee Boy Basin. Follow this road for a tenth of a mile, then turn right onto the entrance road for Box Canyon Falls. You may also wish to continue up Colorado 361 to enjoy the scenery on the way to Yankee Boy Basin (see site 20). The last few miles before reaching Yankee Boy Basin are too rough for passenger cars.

LEE GREGORY

Ouray is known as the "Switzerland of America."

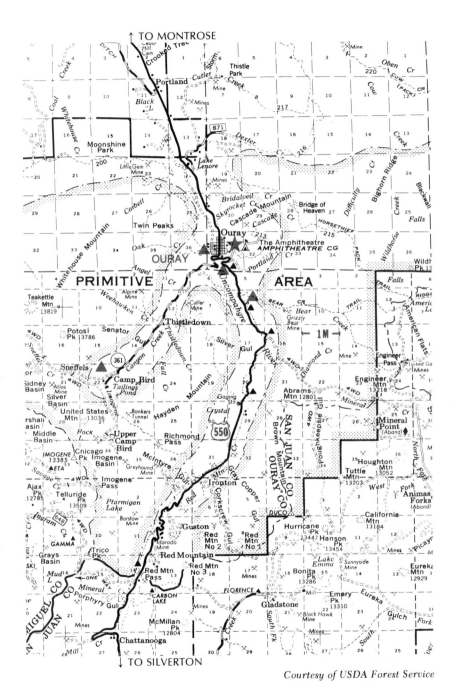

Courtesy of USDA Forest Service

29 ENGINEER PASS

TYPE: Mountain Scenery/Historic
ADMINISTRATION: BLM land/Private land
QUALITY: Superbly scenic
ACCESS: Moderate 4WD
FACILITIES: Rest rooms along Henson Creek
TIME NEEDED: Four hours
BEST VISIT: Midsummer to late summer
BEST PHOTO: All day
ELEVATION: 12,810 feet
REFERENCE: Lake City
MAP: Uncompahgre National Forest visitor map
USGS TOPO: Handies Peak 7.5' (1975)
USGS COUNTY: Hinsdale County Sheet 1 of 2 (1978)
Ouray County Sheet 2 of 2 (1975)
San Juan County (1975)

The drive across Engineer Pass and through its connecting valleys is one of the most scenic trips in Colorado. The route takes you through numerous ghost towns including Capitol City, Rose's Cabin, Engineer City, Animas Forks, and Eureka. There are several buildings remaining at Animas Forks. Please show respect for these mining sites as they are private property or are protected by law. A four-wheel-drive vehicle, which can be rented in Lake City, Silverton, or Ouray, is required to cross the pass where you are treated to a spectacular view of the surrounding jagged peaks of the San Juan Mountains, including several "fourteeners." Passenger cars can negotiate considerable portions of the beautiful connecting valleys. The route from Lake City to Capitol City is particularly rewarding. The directions are given from Lake City to Silverton because it is easier to stay on course in this direction.

DIRECTIONS: From Colorado 149 in Lake City proceed west on a side road <0.0> marked by a green sign that indicates Engineer Pass. Go straight at the stop sign and then turn left at a T-intersection. Follow this good dirt road as it enters Henson Creek Canyon. Continue past two BLM signs <0.2> and the Lake City Mines <3.7>. Go straight at a side road <5.3> leading to Uncompahgre Peak Trail. Pass rest rooms <5.4> and El Paso Creek <7.4> to reach a T-intersection <9.2> at the site of Capitol City. Passenger cars with low ground clearance should go no farther. A BLM sign indicates a left turn for Engineer Pass and a right turn for Uncompahgre Peak. Turn left and then go straight where a side road <9.9> leads to horse corrals on the left. You may wish to stop at Witmore Falls Photo Point <11.1> and follow the short path to an overlook. Continue past Schafer Basin <12.8>, Horseshoe Basin <13.4>, a mining ruin <13.8>, and a rest room <14.5> to reach the site of Rose's Cabin, where the good dirt road ends. High clearance two-wheel-drive vehicles can go this far with no problem but should go no farther.

From Engineer Mountain, you can see Engineer Pass on the right and the surrounding rugged peaks.

The Engineer Pass Road passes through beautiful terrain as it descends toward Silverton.

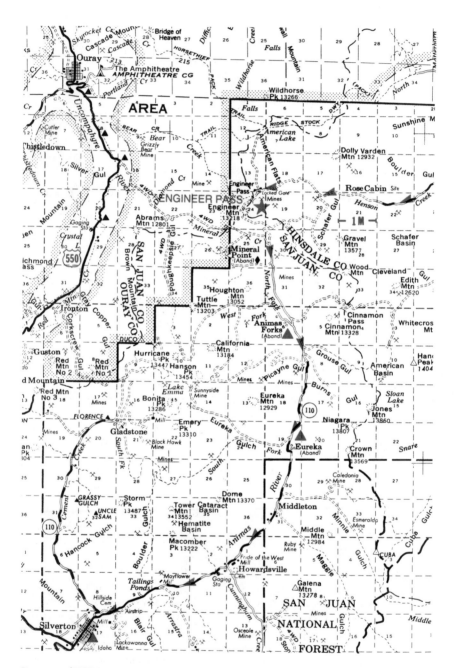

Courtesy of USDA Forest Service

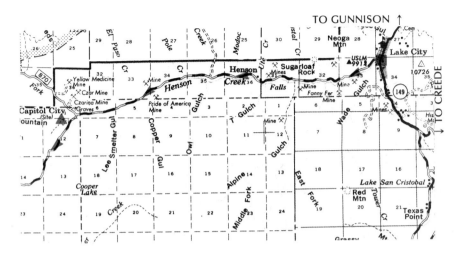

At Rose's Cabin a battered sign <14.6> indicates a right turn for Ouray and Silverton. Four-wheel-drive vehicles should turn right and follow the easy jeep road past Hurricane Basin <15.0>. Bear right where a side road <15.3> joins from the left. Beyond the site of Engineer City <16.0> the route becomes a moderate jeep road as it narrows above timberline. Continue past the Horsethief Trail <17.6> and the Frank Hough Mine <18.3> to reach Engineer Pass <18.5>, marked by a sign.

The main road traverses Engineer Mountain and heads south. It later becomes an easy jeep road after it has left the mountain to descend through the valley. Bear right and continue downhill where a side road <20.0> starts climbing a valley on the left. At a junction <20.9> with a side road, a right turn will take you down a moderate jeep road (Mineral Point Road) 7.2 miles to US 550 where you can turn right to reach Ouray.

To reach Silverton keep left at this intersection. Continue straight where a sign <21.1> indicates a left for Horseshoe Lake. Stay on the main road that descends through the valley as it passes Denver Lake <21.2> and a variety of side roads. Go straight where a side road <21.5> to Mineral Point ghost town joins from the right. A sign marks the junction <22.9> with the Cinnamon Pass Road on the left. The route over Cinnamon Pass is relatively easy and is a scenic alternative return to Lake City (24 miles).

To reach Silverton continue downhill. Bear right at a fork <23.3> to visit the ghost town of Animas Forks <23.6>. Continue on the main road down the valley; ignore the side roads. You will encounter a good dirt road <27.8> at the site of Eureka. Passenger cars from Silverton can come this far. Follow the main road as it continues along the floor of the valley. Go straight where the Stony Pass Road <31.7> joins from the left. The road becomes paved <33.8>, and you should turn left onto Silverton's main street <35.8> to reach US 550 <36.6>.

30 RED MOUNTAIN

TYPE: Mountain Scenery/Historic
ADMINISTRATION: Private land/Uncompaghre National Forest
QUALITY: Very scenic
ACCESS: Paved road
FACILITIES: None
TIME NEEDED: Half hour
BEST VISIT: Spring to fall
BEST PHOTO: Afternoon to late afternoon
ELEVATION: 12,890 feet (Red Mountain Number 3)
REFERENCE: Red Mountain Pass
MAP: State highway map
Uncompahgre National Forest visitor map
USGS TOPO: Ironton 7.5' (1972)
USGS COUNTY: Ouray County Sheet 2 of 2 (1975)

Between Ouray and Silverton, on the Million Dollar Highway northeast of Red Mountain Pass, lies an incredibly colorful ridge known as Red Mountain. Actually, the three major peaks on this ridge are named Red Mountain Number 1 (12,592 feet), Red Mountain Number 2 (12,219 feet), and Red Mountain Number 3 (12,890 feet)—from east to west. The bright reds, yellows, and oranges of Red Mountain are the result of iron oxides, a mineral widespread in this area.

There are also more valuable minerals in the area. The face of the mountain shows the remains of considerable mining activity. Old buildings, roads, tailing piles, and a subterranean network of tunnels still remain. The major mining camps here were Ironton, Guston, and Red Mountain Town. Rich ore was discovered in the late 1870s, and mining activity continued to expand until 1893. The area produced over $30,000,000 in gold, silver, and other precious ores. The mining yield was first shipped over Otto Mears's toll road, now the Million Dollar Highway (see site 32). In 1888 Mears completed a railroad that connected Red Mountain Town with Silverton by going over Red Mountain Pass!

At its peak the population of Red Mountain Town (just north of Red Mountain Pass) was well over 1000. Drinking, gambling, and other establishments were open for business 24 hours a day, but eventually the mining operations ceased and few buildings remain today.

The view of Red Mountain is absolutely spectacular in the late afternoon sunlight. The Million Dollar Highway has numerous turnouts that offer fine views in this area. The tightest curves on the highway can be found just north of Red Mountain Pass (11,018 feet).

DIRECTIONS: Red Mountain can be seen from several turnouts on US 550 just north of Red Mountain Pass. Red Mountain Pass is 11.5 miles south of Ouray and 10.0 miles north of Silverton.

LEE GREGORY

Numerous mining ruins cover the flanks of Red Mountain.

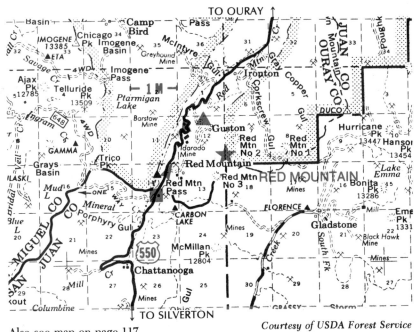

Also see map on page 117.

Courtesy of USDA Forest Service

31 SILVERTON

TYPE: Mountain Scenery/Historic
ADMINISTRATION: Private land
QUALITY: Very scenic
ACCESS: Paved road
FACILITIES: Commercial attractions
TIME NEEDED: Two hours
BEST VISIT: Early summer to fall
BEST PHOTO: Afternoon
ELEVATION: 9,318 feet
REFERENCE: Silverton
MAP: State highway map
San Juan National Forest visitor map
USGS TOPO: Silverton 7.5' (1955)
USGS COUNTY: San Juan County (1975)

Silverton is named for the district's rich mineral reserves. Charles Baker led a prospecting party of six to the Silverton area in the summer of 1860. The first major strike was made in 1870 when a rich gold vein was found in Arrastra Gulch. In 1873 the Brunot Treaty was signed with the Ute Indians, thus opening the San Juans to mining. Within weeks thousands had come to these western mountains. Silverton was platted in 1874, and a string of smaller settlements—Howardsville, Middleton, Eureka, Animas Forks, and Mineral Point—were founded farther north along the Animas River Valley.

During its boom, Silverton's population peaked at just under 4,000. The town, a typical mining camp, had stores, restaurants, a post office, two banks, three hotels, three dance halls, three sawmills, several fraternal lodges, three newspapers, 34 saloons, and the usual gambling and bawdy houses. Schools and churches served the needs of the families living in town. At times Silverton was a rough frontier town. In 1881 the town's marshal, Clayton Ogsbury, was gunned down on a Silverton backstreet.

Silverton was the target of a 270-mile extension of the Denver and Rio Grande Railroad; construction began in 1880. The route headed south from Alamosa, crossed Cumbres Pass (see site 46) into New Mexico, and then continued west to Durango. A 45-mile section was built north from Durango through the deep, narrow canyon of the Animas River. At one point the roadbed was blasted from a sheer cliff face 400 feet above the river. The last rails were laid to Silverton on July 13, 1882. With the railroad's arrival, transportation rates for the silver ores dropped 80 percent. At their peak the surrounding mines shipped $2,000,000 worth of ore annually.

In the 1940s the railroad hauled little freight, and the route may have been abandoned in the 1950s if it were not for the interest of tourists and the work of railfans. In 1962 the 45-mile Durango-Silverton railroad was converted exclusively to tourist traffic. Today a ride on the Silverton train is one of America's most spectacular railroad experiences. During the summer sev-

LEE GREGORY

Silverton rests in the mountain-surrounded valley of the Animas River.

eral round trip trains depart from Durango each day. Advance reservations are strongly advised (see address under Information Sources).

Several Silverton mines are still operating, but it is the town's beautiful setting that attracts the many visitors. Silverton, which still retains its original western flavor, offers shops and services for the vacationer. Four-wheel-drive vehicles can be rented for exploring the surrounding backcountry. The San Juan County Historical Museum is located at the northeastern end of town on Greene Street next to the courthouse. After visiting the town, be sure to drive farther up the Animas River Canyon on Colorado 110. This valley offers dramatic mountain scenery and contains numerous remains of once bustling mining operations.

DIRECTIONS: Silverton is located on US 550, 23 miles south of Ouray and 49 miles north of Durango.

Additional scenery can be enjoyed by following Greene Street, the main road through Silverton, from its junction <0.0> with US 550. Turn right <0.8> onto Colorado 110 (toward Animas Forks, not toward Gladstone). Follow Colorado 110 through the beautiful Animas River Valley past much mining activity and ruins. Passenger cars can continue beyond the end of the pavement <2.8>, past a side road <4.9> on the right to Stony Pass, and as far as the Sunnyside Mill site at Eureka <8.8>.

STATE OF COLORADO

A ride on the Durango-Silverton train is one of America's most thrilling railroad experiences.

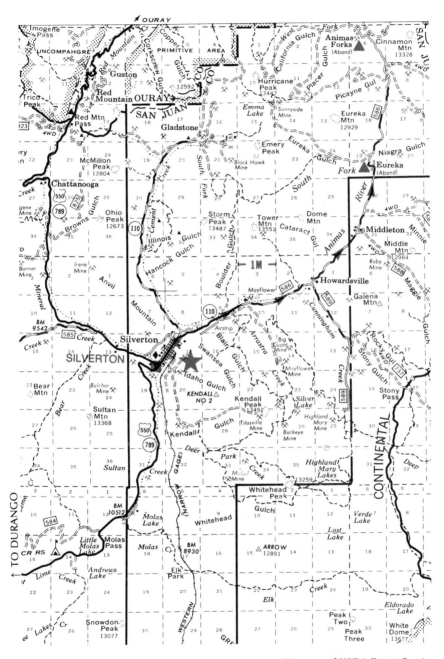

Courtesy of USDA Forest Service

32 MILLION DOLLAR HIGHWAY

TYPE: Mountain Scenery
ADMINISTRATION: Uncompahgre and San Juan National Forests
QUALITY: Extremely scenic
ACCESS: Paved road
FACILITIES: Campgrounds
TIME NEEDED: Two hours
BEST VISIT: Spring to fall
BEST PHOTO: Afternoon to late afternoon
ELEVATION: 10,899 feet (Molas Pass)
REFERENCE: Silverton
MAP: State highway map
Uncompahgre National Forest visitor map
San Juan National Forest visitor map
USGS TOPO: Silverton 15' (1955)
Snowdon Peak 7.5' (1972)
USGS COUNTY: Ouray County Sheet 2 of 2 (1975)
San Juan County (1975)

The Million Dollar Highway is the most spectacular stretch of mountain pavement in Colorado. It traverses a region known as the "Switzerland of America." Some say the route gets its name from the gold-bearing gravel used in its roadbase; others claim its name reflects the high cost of construction. No matter which, its scenery is worth a million.

The route was originally opened in the early 1880s by Otto Mears as a mostly steep, single-lane toll road to handle freight in the rich San Juan mining district. The modern road was constructed in the 1920s, and as a US highway, the road is kept open all year. This is quite a task, and several snowplow operators have been carried to their deaths by avalanches. A few of the numerous scenic spots along the highway are pointed out below.

DIRECTIONS: The Million Dollar Highway is US 550 between Ouray and Silverton, continuing to Durango. Proceed south on US 550 from the southern end <0.0> of Ouray (see site 28). A turnout <1.5> offers good views of Bear Creek Falls (site of the original toll station) and of Abrams Mountain (12,801 feet) to the south. Later, to the north and east are views <9.4> of Red Mountain (see site 30) and the surrounding mining areas. A series of tight switchbacks takes you toward Red Mountain Pass <11.5>. The road then descends through a scenic valley to Silverton <21.5> (see site 31). The highway then climbs past Molas Lake <26.6> (Molas Lake is on private property, please enjoy it from turnouts along the road) to Molas Pass <27.9>. After descending to cross Lime Creek, the road has turnouts <32.9> with views across Lime Creek to the West Needle Mountains. Beyond Coal Bank Pass <35.4> there are views of Engineer Mountain northwest of the highway, then the road continues to Durango <71.4>.

LEE GREGORY

Engineer Mountain is just west of Coal Bank Pass.

LEE GREGORY

Abrams Mountain heads Uncompahgre Gorge.

LEE GREGORY

When the route was first opened, a toll booth was located just above Bear Creek Falls.

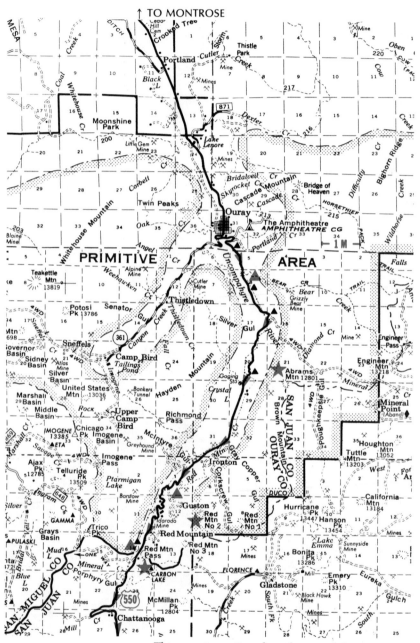

Courtesy of USDA Forest Service This map is continued on the top of the next page.

This map is continued from the bottom of the previous page.

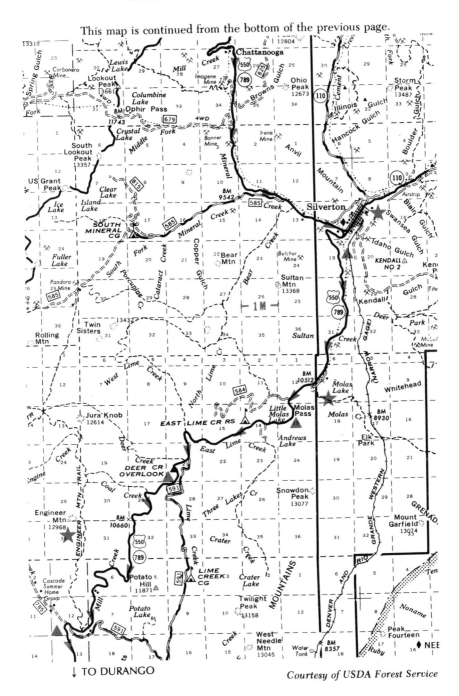

↓ TO DURANGO

Courtesy of USDA Forest Service

CREEDE DISTRICT

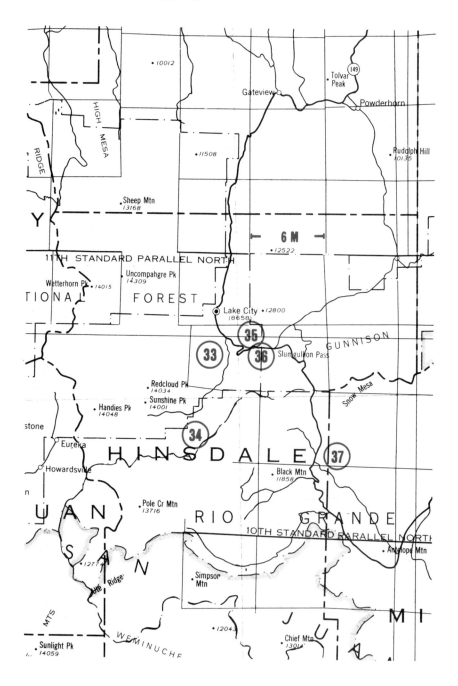

CREEDE DISTRICT

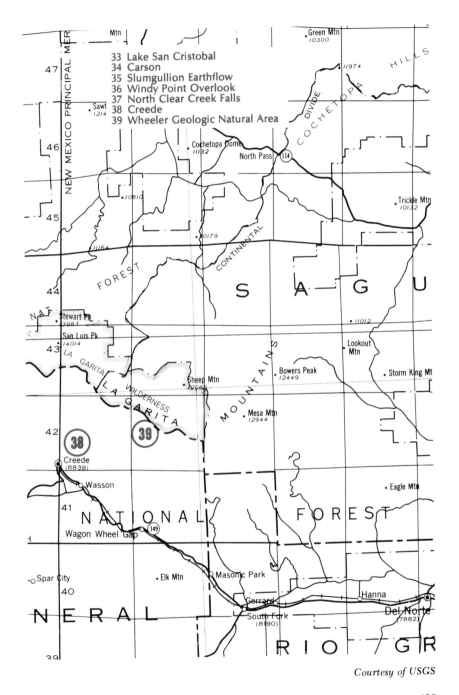

33 Lake San Cristobal
34 Carson
35 Slumgullion Earthflow
36 Windy Point Overlook
37 North Clear Creek Falls
38 Creede
39 Wheeler Geologic Natural Area

Courtesy of USGS

33　LAKE SAN CRISTOBAL

TYPE:	Mountain Scenery/Geologic/Historic
ADMINISTRATION:	Private land/Public land—Hinsdale County
QUALITY:	Scenic
ACCESS:	Paved road
FACILITIES:	Picnic area/Nearby campgrounds
TIME NEEDED:	Half hour
BEST VISIT:	Spring to fall
BEST PHOTO:	Morning
ELEVATION:	8,995 feet
REFERENCE:	Lake City
MAP:	State highway map
	Gunnison National Forest visitor map
USGS TOPO:	Lake San Cristobal 7.5' (1975)
USGS COUNTY:	Hinsdale County Sheet 1 of 2 (1978)

Lake San Cristobal has only existed for 700 years. It was formed when the Slumgullion Earthflow (see site 35) slid into this valley, damming the Lake Fork of the Gunninson River. Water filled the valley behind the slide and overflowed the dam, but the resulting outlet was too small to drain the lake. It is Colorado's second largest natural lake, surrounded by the lofty San Juan Mountains. It is particularly scenic in the fall, with golden aspens and snow-topped peaks.

Just northeast of the lake is Cannibal Plateau, named for the ghastly deed of Alfred Packer. (Packer signed his first name as "Alferd.") Packer, who knew nothing of the territory, offered to guide a small group of prospectors through the Colorado mountains. They departed in November 1873 and became lost in the remote San Juans during the fiercest part of winter. Eventually, Packer wandered into the Los Pinos Indian Agency—alone. People became suspicious, and Packer was arrested. After the winter John Randolph, an illustrator for *Harper's Weekly*, discovered the grisly remains of five individuals, each with flesh cut away, near present Lake City. Packer, jailed in Saguache, escaped the night before the bodies were discovered. Nine years later he was recaptured in Wyoming, returned to Colorado, and sentenced to hang. Packer, Colorado's infamous cannibal, never did hang but spent 17 years in the State Penitentiary.

DIRECTIONS: From the bridge <0.0> over Henson Creek in Lake City, follow Colorado 149 south to a side road <2.2> marked by a sign as access to Lake San Cristobal, Williams Creek Campground, and Cinnamon Pass. Turn right and follow this paved road to Lake San Cristobal <3.5>. You can follow the paved road on the west shore to a day-use picnic area <5.6> and to Williams Creek Campground <9.2>, just beyond the lake. You can also continue south on Colorado 149 for another 0.4 miles to a left turn to reach the Al Packer site marker. Continue on 149 for another 2.4 miles to a turnout on an outside curve with a fine view of the lake.

KEN JESSEN

Lake San Cristobal is Colorado's second largest natural lake.

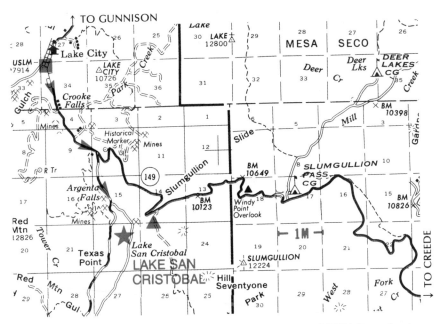

Courtesy of USDA Forest Service

34 CARSON

TYPE: Mountain Scenery/Historic
ADMINISTRATION: Gunnison National Forest/Private land
QUALITY: Very scenic
ACCESS: Easy 4WD or hike
FACILITIES: Nearby campground
TIME NEEDED: One hour
BEST VISIT: Midsummer to late summer
BEST PHOTO: Afternoon
ELEVATION: 11,560 feet
REFERENCE: Lake City
MAP: Gunnison National Forest visitor map
USGS TOPO: Finger Mesa 7.5' (1975)
Lake San Cristobal 7.5' (1975)
USGS COUNTY: Hinsdale County Sheet 1 of 2 (1978)

In 1881 Christopher Carson discovered some promising ore as he was prospecting along the rim of the Continental Divide at the head of Wager Gulch. A mining district was soon organized, and Chris Carson staked claims on both sides of the Divide. The camp, which grew here in 1882, also straddled the Divide and was named Carson in honor of Chris. Silver was the prime attraction, and considerable silver ore was carried down the trail through Wager Gulch and on to Lake City. In 1887 the construction of a wagon road from the south, through Lost Trail Creek, also spurred activity. Both of these trails were dangerous and often impassable. About 150 claims were worked throughout the 1880s.

The silver panic of 1893 nearly killed the town, but a good gold strike was made in 1896. The town peaked in the early 1900s, with as many as 500 men working the site. The mines yielded gold, silver, and copper, with some pockets of ore worth up to $2,000 a ton. The Bonanza King, Chris Carson's claim, was one of the best producers, but it was topped by the Saint Jacobs which produced over $300,000 in ore, $190,000 worth just in 1898. Straddling the Divide meant lots of snow, and little work was done in the winter. Some of the newer buildings were constructed in the 1910s when the Bachelor Mine was active.

Today little remains of the older buildings that stood just below the Continental Divide on both the Atlantic (south) and Pacific (north) watersheds. However, several of the newer buildings, those situated farther below and north of the Divide, are still in remarkably good condition. Fortunately, the townsite is not subject to snowslides, destroyers of many ghost towns. The buildings at this scenic setting are on the edge of a large meadow with a dark background of thick evergreens. To the south is the rim of the Contintental Divide, and to the north is a fine view of Sunshine Peak and Redcloud Peak, both "fourteeners." A four-wheel-drive vehicle is needed to visit Carson, or you can hike the 3.8 miles of jeep road to the townsite. Four-wheel-drive vehicles can be rented in Lake City. Please help

LEE GREGORY

Several buildings mark the site of Carson.

LEE GREGORY

Carson is just below the Continental Divide.

preserve this remarkable slice of history: don't deface or remove any of the property.

DIRECTIONS: From the bridge <0.0> over Henson Creek in Lake City, follow Colorado 149 south to a side road <2.2> marked by a sign as access to Lake San Cristobal, Williams Creek Campground, and Cinnamon Pass. Turn right and follow the paved road along the western shore of Lake San Cristobal past the day-use picnic area <5.6>. Continue on the good dirt road from the end of the pavement <6.3>. Pass a BLM sign <6.4> that identifies this valley belonging to the Lake Fork of the Gunnison River. Continue past the Williams Creek Campground <9.2> to a side road <11.4> on the left, marked by a brown sign that identifies Wager Gulch and a left turn for Carson (4 miles). Passenger cars should park nearby for hiking or may continue straight to enjoy the alternative spectacular scenery of the Lake Fork Valley. Passenger cars can continue at least as far as Sherman (about 3 more miles), the site of an old mining town. Eventually, this road becomes a four-wheel-drive road on the way to Cinnamon Pass.

Four-wheel-drive vehicles and hikers should turn left and start climbing the jeep road toward Carson. This road goes more or less directly to Carson with little opportunity to get lost. As you reach a high meadow with Carson visible on the left, keep left <15.2> and ford a small stream to reach the townsite. The main road continues toward the Continental Divide on the ridge just above Carson.

LEE GREGORY

Iron-stained peaks rise to the north of Carson.

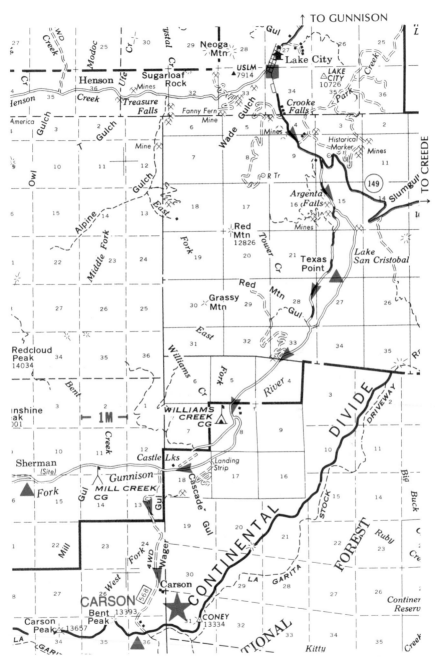

Courtesy of USDA Forest Service

35 SLUMGULLION EARTHFLOW

TYPE:	Mountain Scenery/Geologic
ADMINISTRATION:	BLM land/Gunnison National Forest
QUALITY:	Scenic
ACCESS:	Paved road
FACILITIES:	None
TIME NEEDED:	Half hour
BEST VISIT:	Spring to fall
BEST PHOTO:	Afternoon
ELEVATION:	9,658 feet (road crosses earthflow)
REFERENCE:	Lake City
MAP:	State highway map
	Gunnison National Forest visitor map
USGS TOPO:	Lake San Cristobal 7.5′ (1975)
USGS COUNTY:	Hinsdale County Sheet 1 of 2 (1978)

This region is underlain with poorly consolidated tuff (compressed ash) and breccia (ash mixed with fragments) from an early volcanic epoch. About 700 years ago a large mass of this partially decomposed volcanic rock began to slump from the rim of Cannibal Plateau, named for Alfred (or Alferd) Packer's gruesome deed (see site 33). Excessive rain and runoff probably lubricated the tuff and breccia, initiating the flow. The slide came to rest just as its lower end blocked the Lake Fork of the Gunnison River in the valley below. The resulting lake, Lake San Cristobal, then became Colorado's second largest natural lake. This original earthflow has now become stable; however, its less than solid nature is demonstrated by the bumps in the highway where it crosses the old slide. The main slide descends from an elevation of 11,500 feet to the valley bottom at 8,800 feet. Its length is over four miles, and its width varies from 700 to 1,000 feet. Over 1,000 acres are buried by the bright yellow earthflow.

About 350 years ago a second flow began which now overrides the upper two and a half miles of the old flow. The new flow is still active with a downhill movement of three to twenty feet per year. That's as much as an inch a day, in some portions of the slide. This rate has been measured by placing colored control stakes across the slide in line with two reference points not on the slide. In contrast to the straight, mature trees on the old flow, the trees on the new flow are less healthy, and they lean in various directions. This demonstrates the still active nature of this upper slide. The age of the younger flow was estimated by dating the living trees being carried toward the valley. The slide received its name from a seafaring man who was reminded of slumgullion, a yellow residue from the blubber of a butchered whale.

DIRECTIONS: From the bridge <0.0> crossing Henson Creek in Lake City, proceed south on Colorado 149 as it crosses <4.0> the earthflow and continues to a large turnout <6.0> that offers a close view of the slide.

BUREAU OF LAND MANAGEMENT

The Slumgullion Earthflow slumps in glacier fashion from the rim of Cannibal Plateau to Lake San Cristobal.

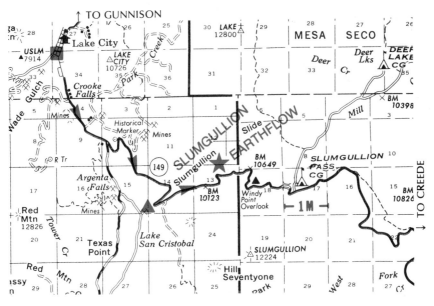

Courtesy of USDA Forest Service

36 WINDY POINT OVERLOOK

TYPE: Mountain Scenery
ADMINISTRATION: Gunnison National Forest
QUALITY: Very scenic
ACCESS: Paved road
FACILITIES: Rest rooms
TIME NEEDED: Quarter hour
BEST VISIT: Spring to fall
BEST PHOTO: Morning
ELEVATION: 10,800 feet
REFERENCE: Lake City
MAP: State highway map
Gunnison National Forest visitor map
USGS TOPO: Bristol Head 15′ (1959)
USGS COUNTY: Hinsdale County Sheet 1 of 2 (1978)

From Windy Point Overlook you can gaze into the majestic high peaks of the San Juan Mountains, Colorado's most spectacular mountain scenery. A sign at the west end of the parking area helps identify the individual peaks of the distant view. To the right, in the far distance, are the most jagged of the San Juan peaks, listed right to left: Uncompahgre Peak (14,309 feet), Matterhorn Peak (13,590 feet), and Wetterhorn Peak (14,015 feet). To the left, from left to right, are Grassy Mountain (12,821 feet), Redcloud Peak (14,034 feet), and the brilliantly-colored Red Mountain (12,826 feet). The cleft below Red Mountain holds Lake San Cristobal, and the edge of the Slumgullion Earthflow can be seen low and to the right.

Uncompahgre Peak is the highest point in the San Juans. All of these peaks are volcanic in origin. Wetterhorn, with its sharp point, was probably the lava conduit of a much larger volcano. Both Redcloud and Wetterhorn were named by the 1874 Wheeler Survey.

Slumgullion Pass, a mile to the east, was crossed by the Hayden Survey of 1874, one of the early mapping missions into the San Juan mining district. Wilson and Rhoda of the Hayden Survey also climbed Uncompahgre Peak that summer. They discovered that grizzly bears had preceded them to the summit. Slumgullion Pass was later the site of a toll road, opened from Del Norte in the late 1870s.

DIRECTIONS: From the bridge <0.0> crossing Henson Creek in Lake City, proceed south on Colorado 149 past the side road <2.2> for Lake San Cristobal (see site 33). Continue as the road crosses <4.0> the Slumgullion Earthflow and passes the Lake San Cristobal Overlook <5.0>. Continue past the turnout <6.0> for the Slumgullion Earthflow (see site 35) to a paved side road <8.2> on the left, marked by a brown sign as Windy Point Overlook. Colorado 149 continues toward Slumgullion Pass <9.9>.

Windy Point Overlook offers a spectacular view into the San Juan Mountains.

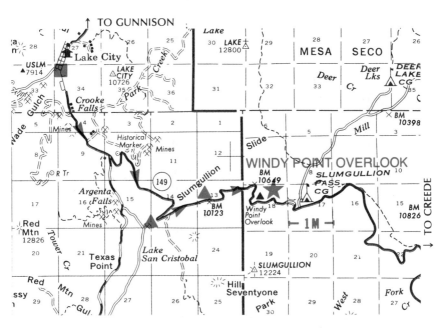

Courtesy of USDA Forest Service

37 NORTH CLEAR CREEK FALLS

TYPE: Mountain Scenery
ADMINISTRATION: Rio Grande National Forest
QUALITY: Very scenic
ACCESS: Good dirt road
FACILITIES: Rest rooms/Picnic area/Nearby campgrounds
TIME NEEDED: Quarter hour
BEST VISIT: July
BEST PHOTO: Morning
ELEVATION: 10,000 feet (top of falls)
REFERENCE: Creede
MAP: Rio Grande National Forest visitor map
USGS TOPO: Bristol Head 15' (1959)
USGS COUNTY: Hinsdale County Sheet 1 of 2 (1978)

North Clear Creek Falls is a picturesque stop just off Colorado 149 about halfway between Creede and Lake City. The falls drop nearly 100 feet into a steep, narrow canyon. At the brink of the falls a block of basalt separates the stream into two plumes that recombine as they crash to the bottom of the canyon.

North Clear Creek gets its start just below the Continental Divide. The creek then meanders across a nearly level, treeless park. This featureless but brush-covered meadow results from the nearly flat underlying basaltic rock formed during an ancient period of volcanic activity. After the falls North Clear Creek continues a few miles to join the Rio Grande River.

The national forest observation site at the falls has a parking area, a fenced overlook, picnic tables, and rest rooms. Campgrounds are located farther along the main dirt road. If you look southeast from the falls, you can see a high, flat, distant plateau known as Bristol Head.

Somewhere between the falls and Bristol Head is the supposed location of Jim Stewart's lost treasure. Stewart, an Army courier, was carrying mail on a route from New Mexico to California in 1852. As the story goes, Stewart was forced to detour through the upper Rio Grande Valley to avoid the local Indians who were on the warpath. Jim's mule supposedly slipped while crossing a stream and dumped the mail bag into the creek. While waiting for things to dry out, Stewart decided to pan the stream bed, and he turned some promising color. He made a careful notation of the location, and upon his arrival in San Francisco he sold the small amount of gold he had discovered. Jim then returned to Colorado and took up residence near Bristol Head. He spent the rest of his life looking for the site of his gold discovery, but for some reason he never found it.

DIRECTIONS: The entrance road <0.0>, marked by a sign, to North Clear Creek Falls is on Colorado 149, 6.5 miles south of Spring Creek Pass and 26.4 miles west of Creede. Follow this good dirt road east and turn left at another sign <0.7> to reach the parking area <0.8>.

LEE GREGORY

North Clear Creek Falls drops from a basaltic rim.

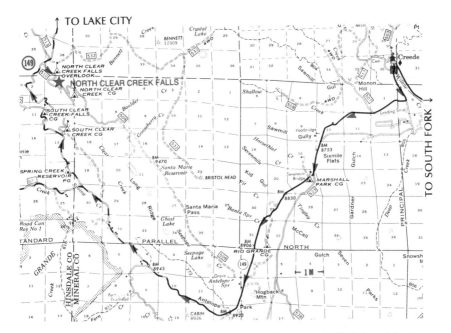

Courtesy of USDA Forest Service

38 CREEDE

TYPE:	Mountain Scenery/Historic
ADMINISTRATION:	Private land
QUALITY:	Scenic
ACCESS:	Paved road
FACILITIES:	Commercial attractions
TIME NEEDED:	One hour
BEST VISIT:	Spring to fall
BEST PHOTO:	Midday
ELEVATION:	8,852 feet
REFERENCE:	Creede
MAP:	State highway map
	Rio Grande National Forest visitor map
USGS TOPO:	Creede 15′ (1959)
USGS COUNTY:	Mineral County Sheet 1 of 2 (1978)

Creede was once one of Colorado's most notorious boom towns. Early prospecting began in the 1870s and '80s, but the Creede rush did not begin until 1890, just after the Holy Moses strike. The town, named for early local settler Nicholas C. Creede, peaked at a population of 10,000, most of whom helped haul out many a ton of rich silver ore. Creede was typical in its mineral wealth, but as a rowdy, wild camp, it had few equals. It was usually controlled by gangsters or confidence men, such as Soapy Smith.

Named after a scam involving bars of soap, Jefferson Randolph "Soapy" Smith unofficially ran Creede during 1892. From his establishment, the Orleans Club, Smith appointed officials and dictated public policy. He later had a similar arrangement at Skagway, Alaska, where he was eventually shot. Another notorious saloon keeper was Bob Ford, slayer of Jesse James. He was shot in his own establishment by Edward O'Kelley. Bat Masterson also ran a saloon in Creede for a while. The spirit of the town was probably best expressed by the last line of an 1892 poem written by Cy Warman, the editor of the town newspaper: "It's day all day in the daytime and there is no night in Creede."

After the silver panic of 1893, Creede fell into decline. Some mining was revived in the 1930s with the production of zinc and lead as well as silver. Today, about 500 people live in Creede where the history and mines remain in the vertical-walled canyons north of town. Summer visitors are attracted by the region's scenery and the fine fishing of the Rio Grande's headwaters.

DIRECTIONS: Creede is located on paved Colorado 149 between Lake City and South Fork. Some of the more dramatic mines of the area can be seen by driving north from the north end <0.0> of town into the narrow canyon. Continue on this good dirt road to the junction <0.7> with a side road to the right (also leads to interesting mines). Take the left fork and continue another quarter mile until a series of mines suspended from top to bottom of a large cliff can be seen.

LEE GREGORY

Many mines line the canyon walls north of Creede.

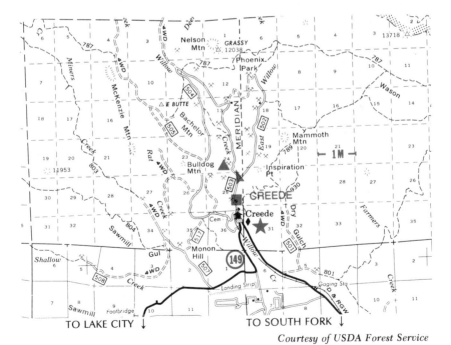

Courtesy of USDA Forest Service

39 WHEELER GEOLOGIC NATURAL AREA

TYPE: Mountain Scenery/Geologic
ADMINISTRATION: Rio Grande National Forest
QUALITY: Extremely scenic
ACCESS: Good dirt road and hike
FACILITIES: Rest rooms at Hanson's Mill
TIME NEEDED: Eight hours
BEST VISIT: Midsummer to late summer
BEST PHOTO: Morning to midday
ELEVATION: 11,959 feet
REFERENCE: Wagon Wheel Gap
MAP: Rio Grande National Forest visitor map
USGS TOPO: Creede 15' (1959)
Pool Table Mountain 7.5' (1967)
USGS COUNTY: Mineral County Sheet 1 of 2 (1978)

Wheeler Geologic Natural Area was once one of the best known and most visited scenic attractions in Colorado. The earliest visitors were Ute Indians who called the area the "sand stones"; renegades used it as a hideout. John C. Fremont was probably the first early explorer to see the area during his search for a reasonable transcontinental railroad route in 1848. It was, however, named in honor of another explorer, Lieutenant George Montague Wheeler, who organized a military survey of the Southwest, including this part of Colorado. From reports of the area by the Wheeler Survey, the fame of this scenic wonder grew throughout the 1870s. After all, the site was a mere eight-mile horseback ride from the growing mining settlements near Creede. Since everything in Colorado was reached by horseback in that period, it was not considered a remote location. Its popularity grew through the turn of the century until it was perhaps the second most visited scenic area in Colorado, topped only by Pikes Peak.

In 1908 the area was designated as Wheeler National Monument by President Theodore Roosevelt. The 640-acre monument, which included about 60 acres of actual formations, was administered by the Forest Service until 1933 when its responsibility was transferred to the Department of the Interior. It was the popularity of the automobile during the 1920s and '30s that led to the downfall of the monument. An automobile road was never built, and so eventually the site became remote by modern standards. The dwindling visitation caused the area to be withdrawn as a national monument, and it was returned to the administration of the Forest Service in 1938.

Wheeler is probably the most interesting geologic scenery in Colorado. It consists of wildly eroded light-gray volcanic tuff, a fine ash that has been compressed into rock. The area includes crevices, ledges, shelter caves, spires, domes, pinnacles, cliffs, narrow canyons, and balanced rocks. These features have been called "The White-Shrouded Ghosts," "Phantom Ships," "Dante's Lost Souls," and "The City of Gnomes." The formations invite you

LEE GREGORY

Strange and exotic forms fill Wheeler Geologic Natural Area.

LEE GREGORY

Compressed volcanic ash has eroded into these spectacular shapes.

to spend many hours of exploration and offer unlimited photo opportunities.

Perhaps the easiest way to see Wheeler is to do the round trip hike (14 miles) in a single day (carry topo maps). The trail has little elevation change, and with a light pack the distance can be covered quickly (about three hours each way). The area is also reached by a difficult jeep road that is 14 miles long, muddy, boggy, and impassable when wet, which is its usual condition. It is faster, easier, and more enjoyable to hike.

DIRECTIONS: Pool Table Road, 7.2 miles east of Creede and 14.0 miles west of South Fork, is marked by a sign where it leaves Colorado 149 between mile-markers 14 and 15. Turn east onto graveled Pool Table Road <0.0> and pass a Forest Service sign that gives mileages to Alder Road (9 miles), Hanson's Mill (10 miles), and Wheeler Geologic Area (24 miles). The road, marked as Forest Route 600, begins to climb to the top of a level plateau above the Rio Grande Valley. The road offers a view <5.7> into this valley and then passes a sign <6.1> identifying Blue Park. Continue straight at a junction <6.5> with a side road on the right, marked by a sign as Blue Park Road. Again, go straight at an intersection <8.9> with Alder Road on the right, marked by a sign as Forest Route 610. This sign also identifies Hanson's Mill as straight ahead, 1 mile. The graveled road ends <9.7> at a sign labeled: Wheeler Geologic Area straight, Wheeler Trail left, West Alder Trail right. A rest room is to the right of this sign, and a sawdust pile (the remains of Hanson's Mill) is on the left. A jeep road continues straight from here.

Leave your vehicle at Hanson's Mill and begin hiking along the jeep road. Soon you will come to a sign < 10.0> that says: To Wheeler Geologic Area, 4WD Road straight ahead, Wheeler Trail to the left. Turn left and follow the road to a sign < 10.1> identifying Wheeler Trail Road (road ends 1 mile), East Bellows Creek (2 miles), and Wheeler Geologic Area (7 miles). Follow this road to its end, and continue on the trail as it eventually drops to East Bellows Creek. It may be best to go downstream a little to find a good crossing. Once you have crossed, follow the creek upstream along the trail on its left bank. You will eventually come to a small sign marking the correct direction with a left arrow. From here the trail leads uphill through a small, usually dry side-canyon on the left side of East Bellows Creek. Continue to a fairly level area devoid of trees. The trail then continues through the remains of a burn and through a stand of trees. Next, the trail opens onto Silver Park which is a long open area between stands of trees. In Silver Park the trail becomes indistinct, but the correct path is marked by a series of top-notched posts set in the rocky soil. Follow these posts across the long dimension of Silver Park until you rejoin the jeep road at a stand of trees on the right. From here it is about a mile to the boundary of the geologic area. Follow the jeep road to the northwest as it winds through another stand of trees. The road ends shortly thereafter in an open area. The trail leads downhill and crosses through a fence marking the boundary of the geologic area. From here it is about 0.6 miles to the formations. After crossing a small, spring-fed tributary of West Bellows Creek, the trail continues uphill toward the light-colored rocks of the geologic area. A small shelter can be found at the base of the eastern formations, and numerous trails wander through the eroded tuff. One trail forms a full loop around the area as well as providing access to Half Moon Pass which crosses the Continental Divide into the La Garita Wilderness.

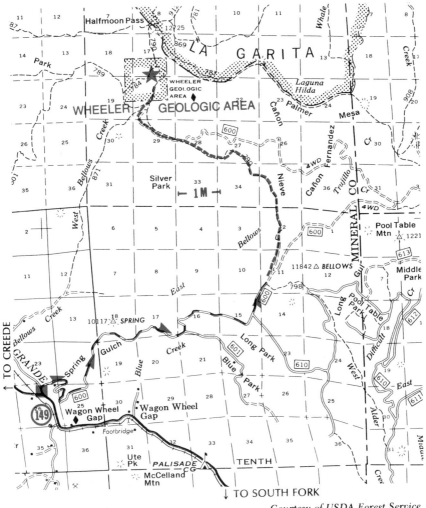

Courtesy of USDA Forest Service

DEL NORTE DISTRICT

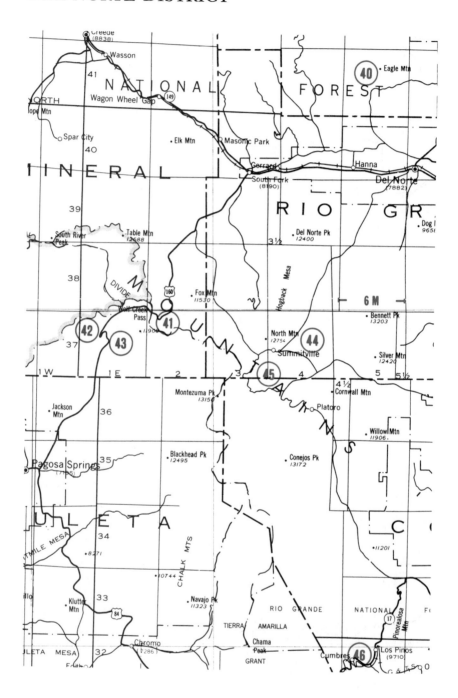

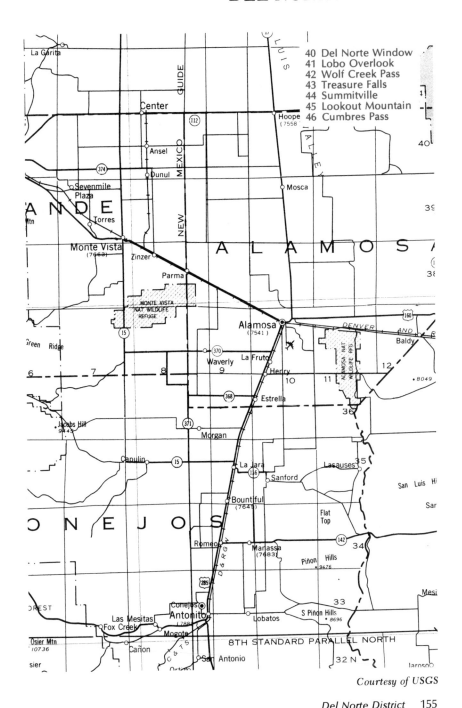

40 Del Norte Window
41 Lobo Overlook
42 Wolf Creek Pass
43 Treasure Falls
44 Summitville
45 Lookout Mountain
46 Cumbres Pass

Courtesy of USGS

40 DEL NORTE WINDOW

TYPE: Geologic Scenery
ADMINISTRATION: Rio Grande National Forest
QUALITY: Scenic
ACCESS: Dirt road
FACILITIES: None
TIME NEEDED: Half hour
BEST VISIT: Spring to fall
BEST PHOTO: Afternoon
ELEVATION: 8,880 feet
REFERENCE: Del Norte
MAP: Rio Grande National Forest visitor map
USGS TOPO: Twin Mountains 7.5′ (1967)
Twin Mountains SE 7.5′ (1967)
USGS COUNTY: Saguache County Sheet 3 of 5 (1979)
Saguache County Sheet 4 of 5 (1979)

The Del Norte Window, also known as La Ventana (Spanish for window), is a large natural opening in a narrow, vertical dike of volcanic lava. This is but one of many volcanic features in the region north of Del Norte. The area, known to geologists as the Summer Coon Volcanic Center, became active about 30 million years ago as the San Juan Range, also of volcanic origin, began building to the west. The Summer Coon Volcano, once as much as eight miles across, has since cooled and been reduced by erosion to the lava plugs, shafts, and dikes that remain today. The Del Norte Window was formed in one of these remaining dikes by the forces of erosion.

The easterly view through the Del Norte Window shows Eagle Rock, a large lava plug named for its nesting sites of golden eagles. Also in this general area evidence can be found of Colorado's earliest inhabitants. Sites have been located which contained small stone structures, Folsom (spear) points, and petroglyphs (rock art). These earliest camps were probably occupied more than 10,000 years ago.

DIRECTIONS: From the junction <0.0> of Colorado 112 and US 160 in Del Norte, proceed north and then east on Colorado 112. Turn left onto a good dirt road <3.2> marked by a sign indicating a turn for La Garita. Continue north on this road (Rio Grande County 33, also marked as road 38A), ignoring the side roads leading east and west. Turn left at a junction <9.2> with a dirt road (muddy when wet), marked by a sign, "Natural Arch, 6 miles." Continue past the Rio Grande National Forest sign on this road (Forest Route 660, also marked as road A32) to a junction <13.1> with a sometimes bumpy dirt road to the right (north). Turn right onto this road which is marked by a sign as "Natural Arch, La Ventana, 1 mile" and follow it to a small loop <14.7>. The window is uphill to the right (east).

LEE GREGORY

The Del Norte Window is a natural arch
in a volcanic dike.

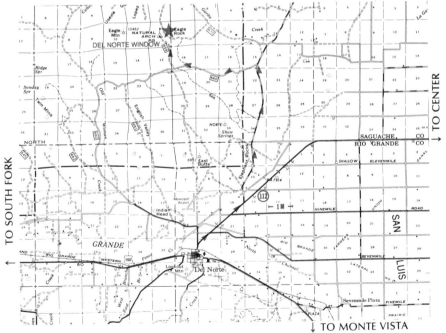

Courtesy of USDA Forest Service

41 LOBO OVERLOOK

TYPE: Mountain Scenery
ADMINISTRATION: Rio Grande National Forest
QUALITY: Scenic
ACCESS: Good dirt road
FACILITIES: Picnic area/Rest rooms
TIME NEEDED: Quarter hour
BEST VISIT: Early summer to fall
BEST PHOTO: Morning
ELEVATION: 11,760 feet
REFERENCE: South Fork
MAP: Rio Grande National Forest visitor map
USGS TOPO: Wolf Creek Pass 15' (1957)
USGS COUNTY: Mineral County Sheet 2 of 2 (1978)

Lobo Overlook is cleverly named. It is directly above Wolf Creek Pass, and *lobo* is Spanish for wolf. This overlook, high atop Thunder Mountain, provides impressive vistas into the surrounding San Juan Mountains. To the south is Treasure Mountain (see site 43), to the far southeast is the Summitville mining district (see site 44), and to the northwest is Sawtooth Mountain. The Continental Divide passes through Lobo Overlook. Drainage to the west goes to the Pacific via the San Juan and Colorado rivers; drainage to the east goes to the Atlantic via the Rio Grande River. You may notice the windswept condition of the trees, as the overlook is at timberline. Also, look for the small alpine flowers that bloom during the summer months just below the overlook's railing. There are benches for the sightseer, picnic tables, and rest rooms at the northern end of the parking area.

Lobo Overlook also marks the southeastern boundary of the Weminuche Wilderness, the largest wilderness area in Colorado at 405,031 acres. It is also Colorado's most popular wilderness area with over 225,000 visitor-days spent here each year. There are over 250 miles of trails inside Weminuche, which has an average elevation above 10,000 feet. Numerous peaks reach 13,000 feet, and the western end of the wilderness contains Windom Peak, Sunlight Peak, and Mount Eolus, three of the most rugged "fourteeners" in Colorado.

DIRECTIONS: Wolf Creek Pass, 23 miles west of Pagosa Springs and 20 miles east of South Fork, is a Continental Divide crossing on US 160. From the summit <0.0> of Wolf Creek Pass (marked by a sign on the south side of the road), proceed east on US 160 a short distance to a marked side road <0.3> on the left. Turn left and follow this gravel road, which soon becomes a dirt road, to the top of the mountain. At the top, just before the main road reaches a microwave repeater station, turn left into the parking area <2.9> for the overlook. Walk to the southern end of the parking area to find a short path leading to the overlook's railing.

LEE GREGORY

The Continental Divide heads northwest from Lobo Overlook into the
Weminuche Wilderness.

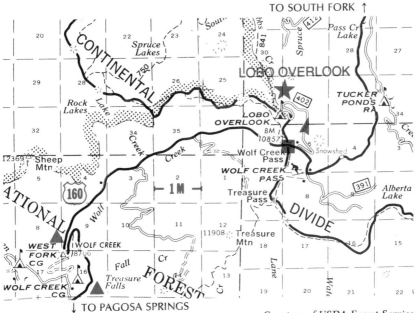

Courtesy of USDA Forest Service

Also see maps on pages 164, 165, and 168.

42 WOLF CREEK PASS

TYPE: Mountain Scenery
ADMINISTRATION: San Juan National Forest
QUALITY: Very scenic
ACCESS: Paved road
FACILITIES: Nearby campgrounds
TIME NEEDED: Half hour
BEST VISIT: Spring to fall
BEST PHOTO: Morning to midday
ELEVATION: 10,850 feet
REFERENCE: South Fork
MAP: State highway map
San Juan National Forest visitor map
USGS TOPO: Wolf Creek Pass 15' (1957)
USGS COUNTY: Mineral County Sheet 2 of 2 (1978)

Traveling over Wolf Creek Pass is a dramatic experience, despite the major United States highway crossing it. From South Fork the road starts climbing through pleasant mountain scenery and passes numerous fishing spots and cascading streams. Near the top you drive under a concrete avalanche chute, designed to keep the annual winter snowslides from sweeping travelers off the road. The Wolf Creek Pass Ski Area, just east of the pass, is seldom short of snow, considering an average of 364 inches falls here each winter. In fact, Wolf Creek Pass holds the Colorado record for a single season's snowfall: 837 inches during the winter of 1978-79.

From Wolf Creek Pass just below Lobo Overlook (see site 41), the highway descends along Wolf Creek to an overlook with a spectacular view of the valley of the West Fork of the San Juan River. The highway drops via a series of switchbacks and passes Treasure Falls (see site 43) on its way to Pagosa Springs, site of a large mineral hot spring.

The area was visited by mountain men as early as the 1820s, and the Hayden Survey mapped the pass during the mid-1870s. However, it was too rough to be used by the early travelers. To the south soldiers built a road over Ellwood Pass in 1878 to reach the new fort at Pagosa Springs. Travelers used this route until it was washed out in the flood of 1911, but the most popular way to reach Pagosa Springs was on the railroad route over Cumbres Pass (see site 46). Construction began in 1913 on a road over Wolf Creek Pass. Completed in 1916, the narrow, hair-raising dirt road had turnouts to allow passing. Today's modern highway is much improved.

DIRECTIONS: Wolf Creek Pass, 23 miles west of Pagosa Springs and 20 miles east of South Fork, is a Continental Divide crossing on US 160. To reach Wolf Creek Pass Overlook, proceed west on US 160 from the summit <0.0> of Wolf Creek Pass (marked by a sign). Where the highway turns to the left at a switchback (just west of mile-marker 161), turn right into a parking area <6.2>, identified by a blue "scenic overlook" sign.

LEE GREGORY

Wolf Creek Pass Overlook offers a fine view of the San Juan River Valley.

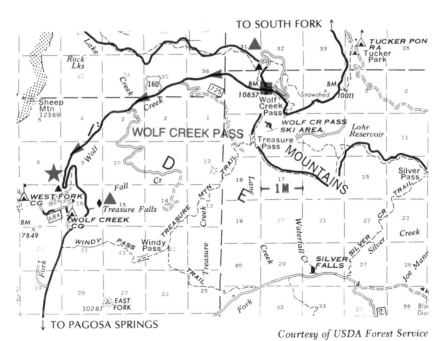

Courtesy of USDA Forest Service

Also see maps on pages 164, 165, and 168.

43 TREASURE FALLS

TYPE: Mountain Scenery
ADMINISTRATION: San Juan National Forest
QUALITY: Very scenic
ACCESS: Paved road
FACILITIES: Rest rooms
TIME NEEDED: Half hour
BEST VISIT: July
BEST PHOTO: Afternoon
ELEVATION: 8,400 feet
REFERENCE: Pagosa Springs
MAP: State highway map
San Juan National Forest visitor map
USGS TOPO: Wolf Creek Pass 15′ (1957)
USGS COUNTY: Mineral County Sheet 2 of 2 (1978)

Treasure Falls is a beautiful cascade on Fall Creek which descends from Treasure Mountain. The falls run most of the year, dropping grandly across the face of a rough volcanic cliff. A legend which holds that $5,000,000 worth of lost gold is buried somewhere nearby is the source of the mountain's name.

As the story goes, a French expedition—including 300 skilled men, 500 horses, and considerable supplies and equipment—set out from Kansas around 1790 to explore the mineral resources of France's Louisiana Territory. They wandered through the Colorado mountains in search of gold, but it was not until reaching the Wolf Creek Pass area that they found enough to set up a permanent camp. Despite being in Spanish territory, they mined a large amount of gold which they stored as bars. The party even wintered in Taos, New Mexico, telling the Spanish that they had been north, surveying French territory.

During their stay in the wilderness, two-thirds of the expedition supposedly died from disease and hardship. The 100 remaining men eventually made plans to return to France, but just as the group was beginning their departure, a band of hostile Indians attacked. During the ensuing battle, the gold was buried on the slopes of Treasure Mountain, and detailed maps were hurriedly made. All but five were killed in the attack or by the long journey to the eastern plains. On the trip across the plains to Kansas, three men drew short straws and were eaten by their companions as a last resort against starvation. The two remaining men reached the French outpost, but one soon died, leaving only the expedition's historian alive.

The historian gave a copy of the map to the French government and kept a copy for himself. The Louisiana Territory was sold to the United States, and 40 years passed before another expedition was organized. It is not known whether this mission was sponsored by France or by the historian's family, but whichever, the group eventually arrived at Taos, New Mexico, where they acquired the services of a Spanish guide. Apparently the party spent as

LEE GREGORY

The ribbon of Treasure Falls drops over jagged volcanic rock.

many as three summers in the area searching for the lost gold with no success.

The expedition left Taos for another season of searching, but their guide soon returned alone, claiming that the group had been wiped out in an Indian attack. The Spanish government accused the guide of murder, but he was acquitted at his trial. It is not known whether the party had actually been attacked or secretly returned to France, having found the treasure.

The guide, as well as descendants of the original expedition's historian, are reported to have later searched the area again and again. A group of prospectors supposedly discovered landmarks on Treasure Mountain that correlated with some of the map's notations and even claimed to have found a 20-foot long mine shaft whose entrance was covered with rocks and dirt. But no gold was ever found.

DIRECTIONS: From Wolf Creek Pass <0.0> (see site 42), proceed west on US 160 past Wolf Creek Pass Overlook <6.2>. As you reach the valley floor, there is a turnout <8.0> on the right (west) side of US 160. Here, a sign indicates pedestrian crossing—stop at this turnout and walk across the highway to reach the short path leading to Treasure Falls.

To reach Treasure Falls from Pagosa Springs, head east on US 160 from its junction <0.0> with US 84. Pull off the highway into a turnout <14.3> on the right (east) side of US 160. This turnout is identified by a "point of interest" sign. A short path leads uphill for a close view of the falls.

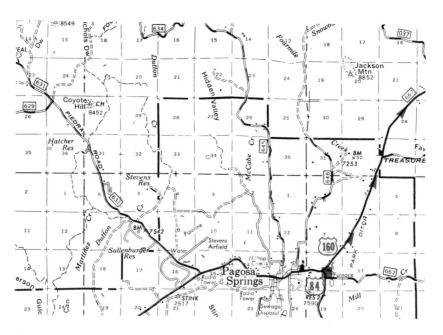

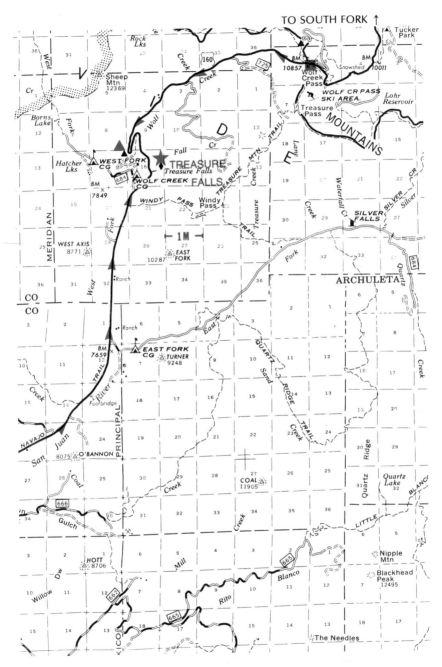

TO SOUTH FORK ↑

Courtesy of USDA Forest Service

44 SUMMITVILLE

TYPE: Mountain Scenery/Historic
ADMINISTRATION: Private land
QUALITY: Scenic
ACCESS: Dirt road
FACILITIES: None
TIME NEEDED: Half hour
BEST VISIT: Early summer to fall
BEST PHOTO: Afternoon
ELEVATION: 11,250 feet
REFERENCE: Summitville
MAP: State highway map
Rio Grande National Forest visitor map
USGS TOPO: Summitville 7.5′ (1967)
USGS COUNTY: Rio Grande County Sheet 1 of 2 (1978)

In 1870 a group of midwestern friends—Baker, French, Reese, Boran, and the Wightman brothers—met in Santa Fe. By early summer they had found their way into this remote section of the southern San Juans without the aid of a guide, and their prospecting soon yielded enough signs of gold to keep them sluicing all summer. Two of the party remained until November and had to wade through waist-deep snow before reaching the Rio Grande and winter safety in New Mexico. The secret of "Wightman's Gulch" leaked out, and when spring returned, so did hundreds of prospectors. "Summit" became the largest camp in the district.

Placer mining yielded to hard-rock mining when veins were discovered in South Mountain at the southern edge of town. Summit soon changed its name to Summitville, the highest incorporated mining town in Colorado. By 1885 the town had over 2,500 staked claims; some, however, were never worked. The population, peaking at about 700, was served by a newspaper, a post office, a boardinghouse, a sawmill, a school, a slaughter house, six processing mills, numerous stores, and at least 14 saloons.

Most of the town's mines are in South Mountain, which has yielded over seven and a half million dollars in silver, copper, and lead, but mostly in gold. South Mountain is volcanic in origin and has undergone changes similar to those of Lookout Mountain (see site 45) to the south. The concentrations of precious metals were deposited in veins during these periods of hydrothermal activity. The richest segment of the mountain measures 4,000 feet long and 1,000 feet wide, and there are over three miles of tunnels inside South Mountain. Some of the best mines were the Esmond, Major, Ida, Golden Star, Yellow Jacket, and Little Annie (the richest), which followed a 17-foot wide vein that produced ores worth $80 to $2,000 a ton.

The boom began to fade in the late 1880s, and the town was nearly empty by 1893. Some of the mines were reopened in 1935, and a significant amount of copper was extracted during World War II. Today, South Mountain, behind the ruins of Summitville, is being worked by the Anaconda Copper

Company. Even though Summitville is private property, you can still view many building remains and scarred South Mountain from the road.

DIRECTIONS: From the summit <0.0> of Wolf Creek Pass (see site 42) on US 160, proceed east to the junction <17.2>. Here a side road on the right is identified by a sign as Park Creek Road and as access to Summitville. Turn onto this dirt road (Forest Route 380), and follow it as it heads generally south, paralleling Park Creek. This is a lightly graveled road. Ignore the side roads until you come to a dirt road <32.2> on the left. Turn left onto this dirt road (Forest Route 330) and follow it east to Summitville <34.9>. Summitville is on private property; please stay away from the mining areas south of the road.

There are alternative access routes to Summitville. You can approach from the east by following the Alamosa River from Colorado 15, or you can approach from the south by following the Conejos River from Colorado 17. Both of these alternatives join near Lookout Mountain (see site 45), then wind west around Schinzel Flats to reach Summitville. Another alternative, Forest Route 330, connects Del Norte with Summitville, but this otherwise fine road is not recommended because of a rough, muddy section of road about 5 miles east of Summitville.

LEE GREGORY

Abandoned buildings mark the site of Summitville.

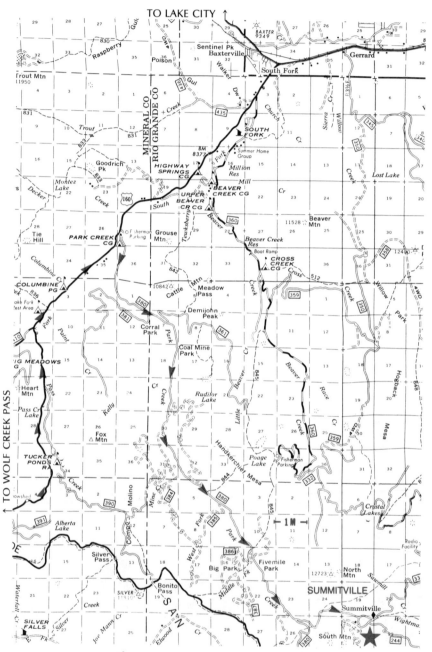

Also see maps on pages 161, 172, and 173.

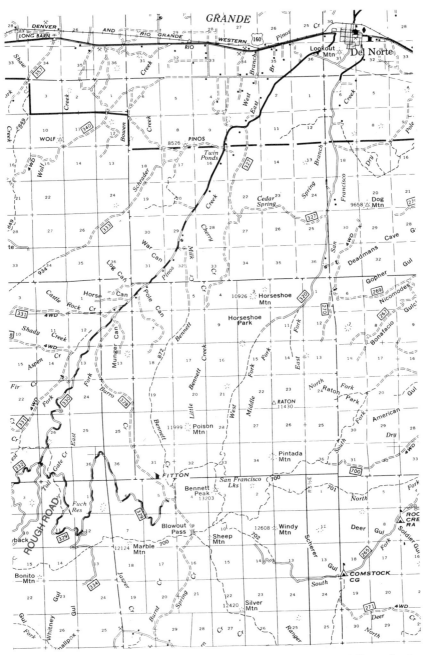

Courtesy of USDA Forest Service

45 LOOKOUT MOUNTAIN

TYPE: Mountain Scenery/Geologic/Historic
ADMINISTRATION: Rio Grande National Forest/Private land
QUALITY: Very scenic
ACCESS: Dirt road
FACILITIES: Nearby campground
TIME NEEDED: Half hour
BEST VISIT: Early summer to fall
BEST PHOTO: Midday to late afternoon
ELEVATION: 12,448 feet
REFERENCE: Summitville
MAP: State highway map
Rio Grande National Forest visitor map
USGS TOPO: Summitville 7.5' (1967)
USGS COUNTY: Conejos County Sheet 1 of 2 (1979)

Lookout Mountain is one of the most colorful peaks in Colorado, especially in the afternoon sunlight. This area was volcanically active about 60 million years ago, and the base of Lookout Mountain was a volcanic vent during the Potosi epoch. The Potosi lava that forms the mountain has since been radically altered by steam, gases, heat, and dissolved chemicals into the present clay-like substance. The erosion-resistant caprock atop Lookout Mouintain, called quartz latite, was laid during a later volcanic period.

The mountain's vivid coloration indicates iron oxides in the rock. Highly toxic substances—compounds of sulfur, calcium, iron, aluminum, and magnesium—are released from Lookout Mountain and similarly colored neighboring mountains by water erosion and flow into the Alamosa River. Hence, the river is too naturally polluted to have fish.

The ghost town of Stunner, on the Alamosa River just below the mountain, was once a small mining town during the 1880s. The mines to the north, near Lookout Mountain, produced some payable ore. A 45-mile toll road was built along the Conejos River from Antonito to help solve the camp's transportation problems. Most of the mines had played out by the 1890s.

DIRECTIONS: From Summitville <0.0> (see site 44) proceed west on the main dirt road (Forest Route 330) to a T-intersection <2.6> with Forest Route 380, where a sign indicates a left turn for Elwood Pass. Turn left and follow the main dirt road. Keep left where the road goes around a privately-owned lake <10.3>. The road offers good views <11.4> of Lookout Mountain. Continue past Iron Creek <11.9> to the junction <14.6> with the Stunner Pass Road, identified by a sign as the way to Platoro (there is an overlook between here and Stunner Pass). From here you can return the way you came, go south through Platoro along the Conejos River to Colorado 17 (see site 46), or go east along the scenic Alamosa River to Colorado 15. Both of these alternative routes are reasonably well-marked.

Lookout Mountain is vividly colored with iron oxides.

45 LOOKOUT MOUNTAIN

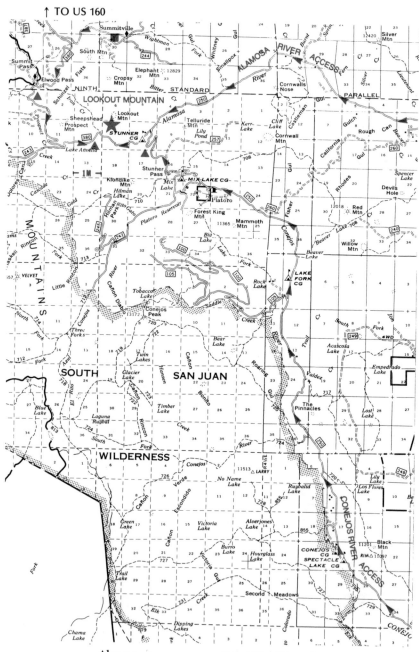

↑ TO US 160

Also see maps on pages 168, 169, 176, and 177.

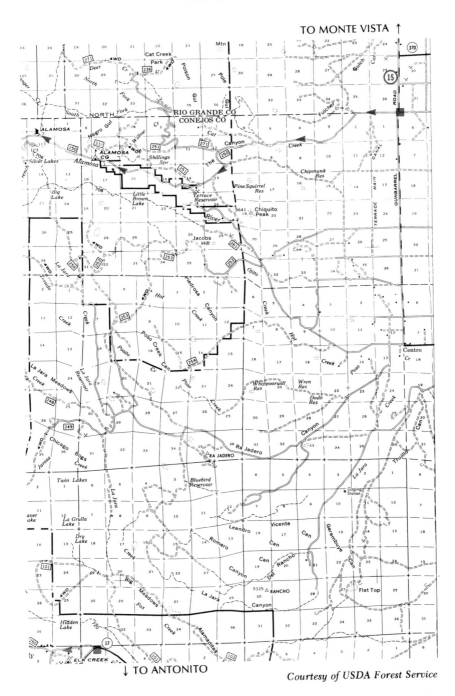

↓ TO ANTONITO

Courtesy of USDA Forest Service

46 CUMBRES PASS

TYPE:	Mountain Scenery/Historic
ADMINISTRATION:	Rio Grande National Forest
QUALITY:	Scenic
ACCESS:	Paved road
FACILITIES:	Nearby campgrounds
TIME NEEDED:	One hour
BEST VISIT:	Spring to fall
BEST PHOTO:	All day
ELEVATION:	10,022 feet
REFERENCE:	Antonito
MAP:	State highway map
	Rio Grande National Forest visitor map
USGS TOPO:	Cumbres 7.5' (1967)
USGS COUNTY:	Conejos County Sheet 1 of 2 (1979)

Cumbres Pass (Spanish for "crests") was first used by Indians and later, during the 16th and 17th centuries, by Spanish explorers, covering the northern bounds of their territory. The original unpaved road across the pass dates from the 1920s. Today a paved highway crosses the pass and opens the scenery of the southern San Juan Mountains to the casual traveler. Cumbres Pass is kept open year-round, despite an annual snowfall of nearly 300 inches.

There is also another way to enjoy Cumbres Pass: narrow gauge rails still cross the pass, and steam locomotives haul trainloads of passengers along this route. In 1879 General William Jackson Palmer decided to build the Silverton extension of his Denver and Rio Grande Railroad by way of Cumbres Pass. This choice was a compromise between difficult alternatives and would provide a 270-mile link between Alamosa and the mines of Silverton (see site 31). The 64-mile mountain railroad begins in Antonito, Colorado, in the flat San Luis Valley and climbs over Cumbres Pass to Chama, New Mexico. This section was completed in 1881, and the full route to Silverton was opened in 1883.

The grade is a gentle 1.4% from Antonito to Cumbres Pass, but the route crosses the Colorado-New Mexico border a dozen times as it curves in and out of south-facing canyons of the Conejos Range. Scenic highlights along this climb are Phantom Curve and Toltec Gorge, the most impressive sight along the entire Silverton extension. The 14 miles of rail from Cumbres Pass to Chama drop at a relatively steep rate of 4%.

In 1970 the 64-mile stretch between Antonito and Chama was bought in a joint preservation effort by the states of Colorado and New Mexico. The line was renamed the Cumbres and Toltec Scenic Railroad. Tickets can be purchased at either Antonito or Chama for sightseeing excursions conducted every day during an extended summer season (reservations are advised: see address under Information Sources).

LEE GREGORY

The Cumbres and Toltec narrow gauge train expells cinders and smoke as it climbs from Antonito toward Cumbres Pass.

46 CUMBRES PASS

Today the modern highway parallels the tracks from a scenic water tank at Los Pinos, about three miles north of Cumbres Pass, all the way to Chama, New Mexico. At the summit of the pass, there is a water tank, a few railroad buildings, and a snowshed-covered "Y" that allows snowplows to turn around. Popular for cross-country skiing, the broad, open meadows at the summit and in the vicinity of Cumbres Pass are the result of a forest fire. The 1878 Osier Mountain fire destroyed 26,000 acres of evergreens. The heat was so intense that trees did not return for nearly fifty years.

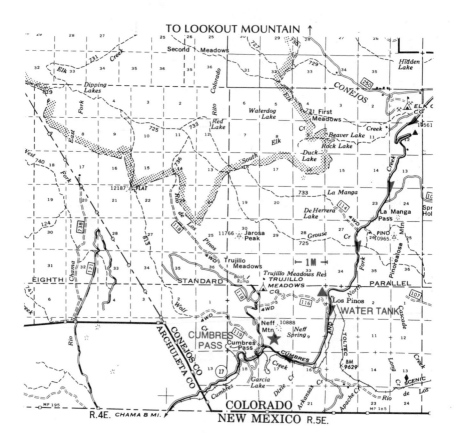

DIRECTIONS: Cumbres Pass (identified by a brass plate in a stone marker) is located on Colorado 17, 4½ miles north of the New Mexico state line and 34½ miles west of Antonito.

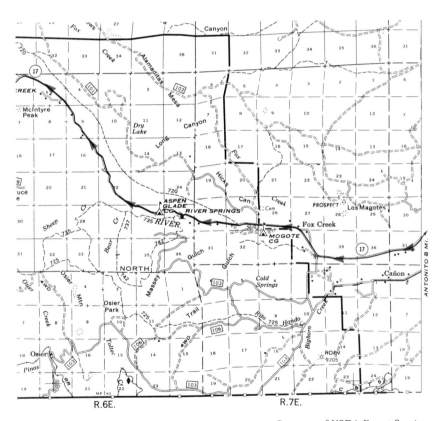

Courtesy of USDA Forest Service

WALSENBURG DISTRICT

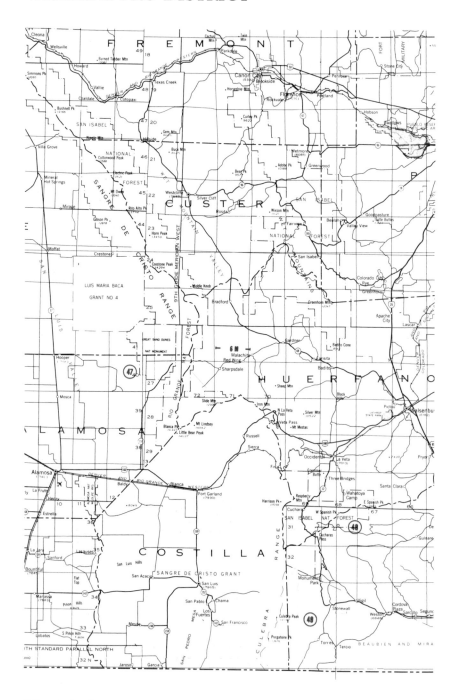

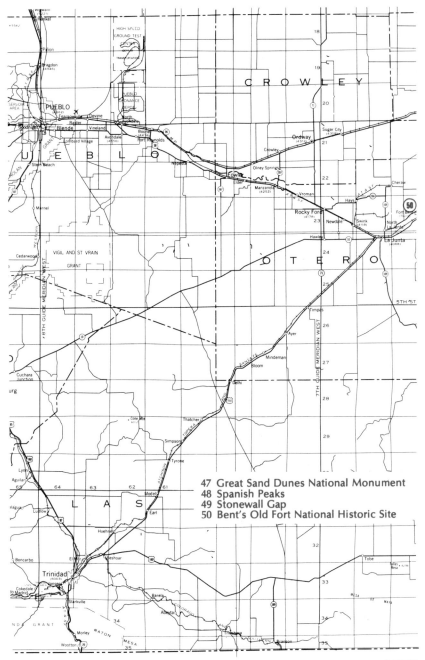

47 Great Sand Dunes National Monument
48 Spanish Peaks
49 Stonewall Gap
50 Bent's Old Fort National Historic Site

Courtesy of USGS

47 GREAT SAND DUNES NATIONAL MONUMENT

TYPE: Mountain Scenery/Geologic
ADMINISTRATION: National Monument
QUALITY: Very scenic
ACCESS: Paved road
FACILITIES: Visitor center/Campground/Picnic areas
TIME NEEDED: Four hours
BEST VISIT: Spring or fall
BEST PHOTO: Morning or afternoon
ELEVATION: 8,175 feet (visitor center)
REFERENCE: Alamosa
MAP: State highway map
USGS TOPO: Great Sand Dunes National Monument (1967) 1:24,000
USGS COUNTY: Alamosa County (1980)
Saguache County Sheet 5 of 5 (1979)

Colorado seems an unlikely place for North America's tallest sand dunes, but they're here in Great Sand Dunes National Monument, rising to nearly 700 feet above the flat, arid grasslands of the San Luis Valley.

This location has the three ingredients necessary for the formation of dunes: sand, wind, and a natural trap. The sand results from erosion of the mountains that surround the broad San Luis Valley. For 15,000 years the predominate southwesterly winds have bounced and rolled grains of sand across the valley floor. As the winds reach the northeast edge of the valley, they encounter an abrupt 4,000-foot wall of mountains known as the Sangre de Cristo Range. As the wind crosses Mosca, Medano, and Music passes, low points in the range, dust may be carried over the mountains, but sand is too heavy. It is deposited in dunes at the curved base of the range.

The winds continue to add to the dunes, which cover a huge area of over 150 square miles, and winds that occasionally blow in reverse, down from the passes, pile the dunes back onto themselves, making them higher. When hiking on the dunes, be sure to carry shoes; the sand can become blistering hot during midday. You should also carry water and a protective lotion against sunburn.

Sites excavated near the dunes reveal that Folsom Man camped here about 10,000 years ago. Zebulon Montgomery Pike constructed a stockade abut 30 miles to the southwest to serve as a base for his explorations through the winter of 1806-07; he first saw the dunes in January, 1807. Great Sand Dunes became a national monument in 1932.

DIRECTIONS: From Alamosa, proceed 14 miles east on US 160 to a well-marked intersection with Colorado 150. Turn left and continue for 19 miles on paved Colorado 150 to the monument's visitor center.

BUREAU OF LAND MANAGEMENT

Rising 700 feet, North America's tallest sand dunes rest against the
Sangre de Cristo Mountains.

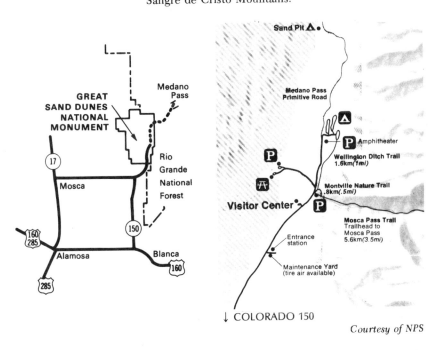

Courtesy of NPS

48 SPANISH PEAKS

TYPE: Mountain Scenery
ADMINISTRATION: San Isabel National Forest/Private land
QUALITY: Scenic
ACCESS: Paved road
FACILITIES: Campgrounds/Picnic areas
TIME NEEDED: One hour
BEST VISIT: Early summer to fall
BEST PHOTO: Afternoon to late afternoon
ELEVATION: 13,626 feet (West Spanish Peak)
REFERENCE: La Veta
MAP: State highway map
San Isabel National Forest visitor map
USGS TOPO: Spanish Peaks 7.5' (1971)
Cuchara 7.5' (1963)
Cucharas Pass 7.5' (1967)
Herlick Canyon 7.5' (1971)
USGS COUNTY: Huerfano County Sheet 4 of 4 (1975)
Las Animas County Sheet 4 of 7 (1978)

The Spanish Peaks, or Las Cumbres Españolas, were once crucial land-marks marking the bounds between the seemingly endless eastern plains and the southern Rocky Mountains. The peaks stand apart from the main ranges to the west and rise more than 7,000 feet above the Great Plains. Long before Zebulon Montgomery Pike sighted the peak that now bears his name, the Spanish Peaks were guiding Indians, Spanish, and French trappers to the settlements of New Mexico.

These twin mountains held a religious significance for the Ute, Comanche, Apache, and other nearby plains tribes. Summer thunderstorms, which typically cluster around the isolated peaks, were evidence that the rain gods made their home on the Spanish Peaks. The Indians called these mountains Wahatoya, or "Breasts of the World." Ancient Aztec records were found in Mexico that referred to mountains of this name as a source of gold.

The first recorded Europeans to visit Colorado were the Spanish. In 1694 Diego de Vargas, Governor of Spanish New Mexico, led an expedition into the San Luis Valley, just west of the peaks. In 1706 the first recorded journey past the peaks was led by Juan de Ulibarri who was traveling north from Santa Fe. One of the most notable Spanish explorers was Governor Juan Bautista de Anza, the founder of San Francisco. In 1779 De Anza led a force north from New Mexico into the San Luis Valley, across Poncha Pass, through South Park, and east to the plains. He then attacked the Comanches from the north, near present Colorado City, where their chief, Cuerno Verde, and many warriors were killed. The peaks later marked the way for American explorers and were important landmarks on the Santa Fe Trail.

The Spanish Peaks are igneous intrusions, molten rock that was injected into surrounding sedimentary rock. The sedimentary rock has been re-

LEE GREGORY

The Cordova Pass Scenic Drive goes through this tunnel in a volcanic dike.

moved by erosion, exposing the peaks. Numerous volcanic dikes, formed when molten rock filled cracks and fissures in the sedimentary rock, radiate from the peaks. As the surrounding sediments were eroded, the dikes were left standing as long, thin, isolated walls. Over 400 separate dikes have been identified, with widths ranging from one to 100 feet. This geology combines to form interesting, dramatic scenery.

DIRECTIONS: From the town of La Veta <0.0> (south of US 160 between La Veta Pass and Walsenburg), proceed south on Colorado 12, which offers views of the Spanish Peaks to the east and passes several volcanic dikes, including the Devil's Staircase <6.4>. Continue past a San Isabel National Forest sign <12.4> to reach Cucharas Pass <17.3>, identified by a sign. Colorado 12 continues south past North Lake <25.0>, Monument Lake <27.9>, and Stonewall Gap <32.2> (see site 49).

Some of the best views of the peaks are from the Cordova Pass Scenic Drive. This dirt road leaves from the summit <0.0> of Cucharas Pass and heads east toward Cordova Pass <6.0> (shown as Apishapa Pass on some maps), marked by a sign. The road descends past a good view <6.5> of the peaks before it reaches an interesting tunnel <9.6> through a volcanic dike. The road then leaves San Isabel National Forest and continues for another 24 miles before reaching Interstate 25 at Aguilar. After visiting the tunnel, you may wish to return to Colorado 12, since the lower portions of this dirt road become muddy when wet.

LEE GREGORY

The Devil's Staircase is but one of many dikes radiating from the Spanish Peaks.

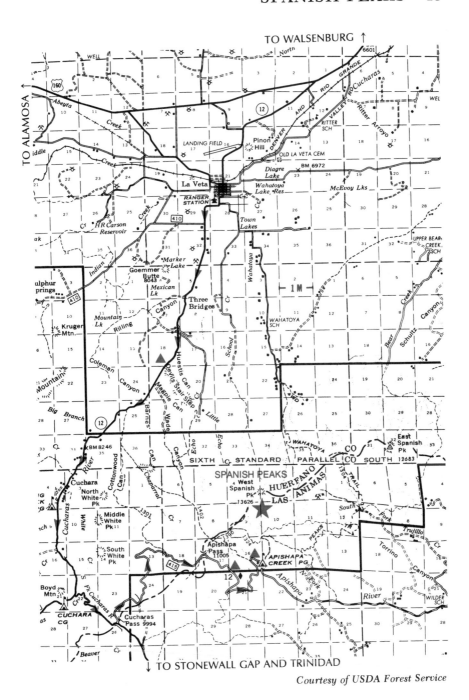

Courtesy of USDA Forest Service

49 STONEWALL GAP

TYPE: Foothills Scenery/Geologic
ADMINISTRATION: Private land
QUALITY: Scenic
ACCESS: Paved road
FACILITIES: None
TIME NEEDED: Quarter hour
BEST VISIT: Spring to fall
BEST PHOTO: Afternoon
ELEVATION: 7,940 feet
REFERENCE: Stonewall
MAP: State highway map
BLM Alamosa 1:100,000
USGS TOPO: Stonewall 7.5' (1967)
USGS COUNTY: Las Animas County Sheet 4 of 7 (1978)

Immediately west of the town of Stonewall is a hogback of sedimentary rock, upturned by the rise of the Culebra Range to the west. This hogback has been tilted so sharply that its erosion-resistant layer of Dakota sandstone stands nearly vertical, forming a natural wall that continues for miles as it parallels the mountains in a north-south direction. Through this stone wall is a cut, Stonewall Gap, caused by stream erosion. Several small creeks join just west of the gap to form the Middle Fork of the Purgatoire River, which then flows east through the gap on its journey toward Trinidad. It eventually joins the Arkansas River near Las Animas in eastern Colorado.

The river's name, "Purgatoire," is a shortened version of its original 16th century christening by Spanish explorers. In the mid-1590s Conquistadores, led by Juan Hermana and Francisco Bonilla, headed north from Mexico in search of the Seven Cities of Cibola. A disagreement between the leaders resulted in the death of Bonilla, and when Hermana continued north, the priest and a few followers returned to Mexico, refusing to continue with the murderous leader. Nothing was heard from the Hermana party until a later expedition discovered their bones on the banks on a river. Massacred by Indians without a priest to administer the last rites, their souls were believed doomed to wander endlessly in purgatory. The river was then named El Rio de las Animas Perdidas en Purgatorio, the river of the souls lost in purgatory.

Colorado 12 passes through Stonewall Gap just before it turns north toward Monument Lake, so named because of a solitary rock protruding from its surface. The best views of the wall and its gap are from its west side along the highway. Please do not trespass.

DIRECTIONS: From Trinidad take the Interstate 25 exit <0.0> for Colorado 12 west. Proceed west on Colorado 12 past the town of Stonewall to Stonewall Gap <32.9>. After passing through the gap, Colorado 12 continues past Monument Lake <37.2> and the Spanish Peaks (see site 48) toward the town of La Veta <65.1>.

The Purgatoire River has cut this gap through a nearly vertical wall of Dakota sandstone.

LEE GREGORY

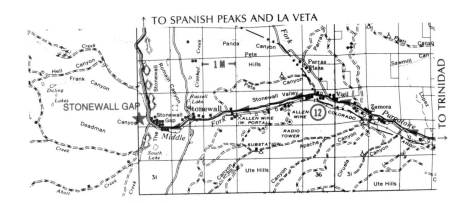

Courtesy of BLM

50 BENT'S OLD FORT

TYPE: Plains Scenery/Historic
ADMINISTRATION: National Historic Site
QUALITY: Scenic
ACCESS: Paved road
FACILITIES: Visitor center/Picnic areas
TIME NEEDED: Two hours
BEST VISIT: Spring or fall
BEST PHOTO: Morning
ELEVATION: 4,005 feet
REFERENCE: La Junta
MAP: State highway map
USGS TOPO: Hadley 7.5' (1976)
USGS COUNTY: Otero County Sheet 1 of 2 (1979)

Bent's Old Fort was constructed along the Arkansas River in 1833-34 by Ceran St. Vrain and two brothers, Charles and William Bent. Their trading post became the most important stop along the Santa Fe Trail, which connected Missouri and Santa Fe, New Mexico. For 16 years, the Bents and St. Vrain managed an influential commercial empire. Posts owned by these men in Santa Fe and Taos, New Mexico, were supplied by goods freighted by way of Bent's Fort from Missouri. Similarly, goods of Mexican and Navajo manufacture were freighted to Missouri. The fort was also a center of trade with the plains Indians, including Cheyenne, Arapahoe, Comanche, and Kiowa. The Bent's bartered for buffalo hides and wielded considerable influence over the tribes. The fort was also a collection point for beaver pelts and a distribution center for supplies to the many independent mountain men who were trapping furs in the Rockies. Military conflict between Mexico and the United States in 1846 and Indian trouble in 1847, prompted by invading settlers, led to the fort's abandonment in 1849.

Bent's Old Fort was excavated and then accurately reconstructed during 1975-76 to reflect its appearance in 1845-46, the zenith of the fort's activity. Virtually all of the rooms have been refurnished, both with antiques and reproductions, many of which were made in the fort's reconstructed blacksmith and carpenter shops. The fort is open to visitors from 8:00 AM to 4:30 PM from September to May and 8:00 AM to 6:00 PM from Memorial Day through Labor Day. During the summer season, costumed interpreters are on duty in the fort to help you enjoy your visit.

DIRECTIONS: In eastern La Junta, a sign marks the turn for Bent's Fort at the junction <0.0> of Colorado 109 and US 50. Turn south onto Colorado 109, go one block, turn left (indicated by a sign to Bent's Fort), go another block, turn left again (indicated by another sign), and cross the bridge over US 50. Continue north on Colorado 109 through a residential area to its junction <1.2> with Colorado 194, marked by a sign indicating Bent's Fort. Turn right and follow Colorado 194 to the fort's entrance <7.6>.

LEE GREGORY

A fur press stands in the plaza of the reconstructed Bent's Old Fort.

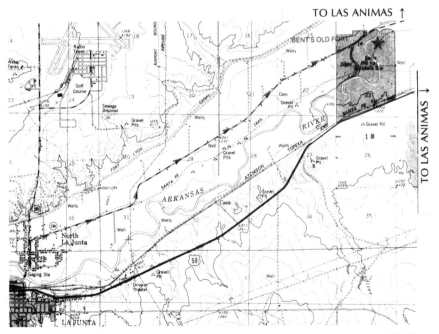

Courtesy of USGS

SUMMARY

DISTRICT	SITE NUMBER AND NAME	SCENERY	ADMIN.	QUALITY	ACCESS	HOURS	VISIT	PHOTO
Grand Junction	1 Miracle Rock	TG	B	S	G	½	SF	MA
	2 Rattlesnake Canyon	TG	B	E	R	4	SF	DA
	3 Colorado National Monument	TG	M	V	P	4	SF	AL
	4 Mount Garfield	TG	B	S	P	¼	SF	AL
	5 Grand Mesa	TG	F	S	D	2	EJLF	D
	6 Unaweep Canyon	TG	X	S	P	1	SF	M
	7 Dolores Canyon	TGH	BX	S	P	1	SF	DA
Gunnison	8 Black Canyon of the Gunnison	TG	M	E	P/G	2	SEJLF	EMDAL
	9 Curecanti Needle	TGH	R	S	P	½	SEJLF	MA
	10 Kebler Pass	MH	F	V	C	2	EJLF	M
	11 Gothic	MH	X	V	C	1	EJLF	A
	12 Timberline Overlook	M	F	S	C	½	JL	M
	13 Tincup	MH	X	S	C	½	EJLF	MD
	14 Cumberland Pass	MH	FX	S	C	1	JL	M
	15 Alpine Tunnel	MH	F	S	R	1	JL	D
Four Corners	16 Dolores Overlook	TG	B	S	G	½	SEJLF	DA
	17 Lowry Pueblo	TO	B	V	G	1	SF	MA
	18 Hovenweep National Monument	TO	M	V	D	2	SF	MA
	19 Mesa Verde National Park	TO	P	E	P	8	SF	EMDAL
Telluride	20 Imogene Pass	MH	XF	*	4	4	JL	EMDAL
	21 Telluride	MH	X	E	P	1	SEJLF	A
	22 Alta	MH	X	V	D	1	EJLF	A
	23 Ophir Pass	MH	F	E	E	2	JL	A
	24 Trout Lake	M	X	V	P	½	SEJLF	A
	25 Lizard Head Peak	M	F	S	P	¼	SEJLF	MD
San Juan	26 Chimney Rock	MG	F	V	G	2	EJLF	A
	27 Dallas Divide	M	X	V	P	½	SEJLF	AL
	28 Ouray	MH	X	V	P	2	SEJLF	DA
	29 Engineer Pass	MH	BX	*	M	4	JL	EMDAL
	30 Red Mountain	MH	XF	V	P	½	SEJLF	AL
	31 Silverton	MH	X	V	P	2	EJLF	A
	32 Million Dollar Highway	M	F	E	P	2	SEJLF	AL

DISTRICT	SITE NUMBER AND NAME	SCENERY	ADMIN.	QUALITY	ACCESS	HOURS	VISIT	PHOTO
Creede	33 Lake San Cristobal	MGH	X*	S	P	½	SEJLF	M
	34 Carson	MH	FX	V	E/H	1	JL	A
	35 Slumgullion Earthflow	MG	BF	S	P	½	SEJLF	A
	36 Windy Point Overlook	M	F	V	P	¼	SEJLF	M
	37 North Clear Creek Falls	MH	X	V	G	¼	J	M
	38 Creede	MH	X	S	P	1	SEJLF	D
	39 Wheeler Geologic Natural Area	MG	F	E	GH	8	JL	MD
Del Norte	40 Del Norte Window	G	F	S	D	½	SEJLF	A
	41 Lobo Overlook	M	F	S	G	¼	EJLF	M
	42 Wolf Creek Pass	M	F	V	P	½	SEJLF	MD
	43 Treasure Falls	M	F	V	P	½	J	A
	44 Summitville	MH	X	S	D	½	EJLF	A
	45 Lookout Mountain	MGH	FX	V	D	½	EJLF	DAL
	46 Cumbres Pass	MH	F	S	P	1	SEJLF	EMDAL
Walsen-burg	47 Great Sand Dunes Natl. Mon.	MG	M	V	P	4	SF	MA
	48 Spanish Peaks	M	FX	S	P	1	EJLF	AL
	49 Stonewall Gap	FG	X	S	P	¼	SEJLF	A
	50 Bent's Old Fort	PH	M	S	P	2	SF	M

SCENERY
M: Mountains
F: Foothills
P: Plains
T: Plateau
G: Geologic
H: Historic
O: Other

ADMINISTRATION
P: Natl Park
M: Natl Monument
R: Natl Rec Area
F: Natl Forest
G: Natl Grassland
B: BLM
U: US Military
*: Public Land
X: Private Land

QUALITY
*: Superbly Scenic
E: Extremely Scenic
V: Very Scenic
S: Scenic

VISIT
S: Spring
E: Early Summer
J: July
L: Late Summer
F: Fall
W: Winter

ACCESS
P: Paved
G: Good Dirt
D: Dirt
R: Rough Dirt
E: Easy 4WD
M: Moderate 4WD
4: Difficult 4WD
H: Hike

PHOTO
E: Early Morning
M: Morning
D: Midday
A: Afternoon
L: Late Afternoon

MAP DATA

Page: Map Name

26, 27: USGS State of Colorado 1:500,000
30, 31: BLM NW-25 Surface Management Quad
34, 35: BLM Grand Junction District Office
39: NPS Colorado National Monument
41, 43: Grand Mesa National Forest Visitor Map
45, 49: Uncompahgre National Forest Visitor Map
50, 51: USGS State of Colorado 1:500,000
54, 55, 57, 60, 61, 63: Gunnison National Forest Visitor Map
65, 68, 69, 71, 74, 75: Gunnison National Forest Visitor Map
76, 77: USGS State of Colorado 1:500,000
79: San Juan National Forest Visitor Map
81: BLM SW-19 Surface Management Quad
83: NPS Hovenweep National Monument
87: San Juan National Forest Vistor Map
88, 89: USGS State of Colorado 1:500,000
93, 97, 99, 101, 103, 105: Uncompahgre National Forest Visitor Map
106, 107: USGS State of Colorado 1:500,000
111: Gunnison National Forest Visitor Map
113, 117, 120, 121, 123: Uncompahgre National Forest Visitor Map
127: San Juan National Forest Visitor Map
132: Uncompahgre National Forest Visitor Map
133: San Juan National Forest Visitor Map
134, 135: USGS State of Colorado 1:500,000
137, 141, 143, 145: Gunnison National Forest Visitor Map
147, 149, 153: Rio Grande National Forest Visitor Map
154, 155: USGS State of Colorado 1:500,000
157, 159: Rio Grande National Forest Visitor Map
161, 164, 165: San Juan National Forest Visitor Map
168, 169, 172, 173, 176, 177: Rio Grande National Forest Visitor Map
178, 179: USGS State of Colorado 1:500,000
181: NPS Great Sand Dunes National Monument
185: San Isabel National Forest Visitor Map
187: BLM SE-21 Surface Management Quad
189: USGS Otero County Sheet 1 of 2

MAP SOURCES

National Forest and National Grassland Visitor Maps:
  Visitor Map Sales
  USDA Forest Service
  P.O. Gox 25127
  Lakewood, Colorado 80225

USGS Maps:
  USGS Map Sales
  Building 810
  Denver Federal Center
  Denver, Colorado 80225

BLM Maps:
  Bureau of Land Management
  Colorado State Office
  2850 Youngfield Street
  Denver, Colorado 80215

NPS Maps:
  National Park Service
  United States Department of the Interior
  12795 W. Alameda Parkway
  P.O. Box 25287
  Denver, Colorado 80225

State Highway Map:
  State Department of Highways
  4201 East Arkansas Avenue
  Denver, Colorado 80222

PHOTOGRAPHIC DATA

Page: Subject and from where taken, source, time of day, month, year.

Front cover: Great Sand Dunes National Monument, Bob Schram, afternoon, August, 1974.

6: Autumn scenery in the San Juan Mountains of southwestern Colorado, State of Colorado: Office of Tourism.

11 top: Satellite photo of Colorado, USGS Conterminous United States NASA ERTS-1, Satellite Image Mosaic, Band 7-Summer, 1974.

11 bottom: Geologic zones of Colorado, Colorado Geological Survey Bulletin 32, *Prairie, Peak, and Plateau*, 1972.

29: Miracle Rock from the north, Steve Reames, morning, May, 1982.

33 top: Large arch in the east rim of Rattlesnake Canyon from the lower level, Lee Gregory, morning, August, 1989.

33 bottom: Major arch in the east rim from above, Lee Gregory, morning, August, 1989.

37 top: The Coke Ovens from the overlook, Lee Gregory, afternoon, August, 1989.

37 bottom: Independence Monument, Colorado Office of Tourism.

41: Mount Garfield from the turnout on Interstate 70, Lee Gregory, afternoon, September, 1983.

43: The rim of Grand Mesa from the south along Lands End Road, Lee Gregory, afternoon, September, 1979.

45: Unaweep Canyon from the east near the Divide Road turnoff, Lee Gregory, midday, July, 1979.

47 top: Hanging Flume on the Dolores Canyon wall from the overlook, Lee Gregory, midday, July, 1979.

47 bottom: Hanging Flume sign at the overlook, midday, July, 1979.

53: The Painted Wall from Painted Wall View on the south rim, Lee Gregory, midday, August, 1981.

57: Curecanti Needle from about a mile east on Colorado 92, Lee Gregory, morning, September, 1989.

59 top: Lake Irwin from the southeast, Lee Gregory, morning, September, 1989.

59 bottom: The West Elk Mountains from the junction of Forest Road 706 and the Kebler Pass Road, Lee Gregory, morning, September, 1989.

63: Gothic from the south, Lee Gregory, midday, September, 1989.

65: Looking north toward the Sawatch Range from the hill north of the overlook, Lee Gregory, morning, August, 1982.

67: Tincup's town hall from the south, Lee Gregory, morning, August, 1982.

71: Ruins of the Bon Ton Mine at the southern base of Cumberland Pass, Lee Gregory, morning, July, 1981.

73 top: Looking south from the old railroad grade toward Tomichi Pass, Ken Jessen, midday.

PHOTOGRAPHIC DATA

73 bottom: The collapsed west portal of the Alpine Tunnel, Ken Jessen, midday.

79: Looking southeast into the Dolores Canyon from the overlook, Lee Gregory, midday, September, 1979.

81: Lowry ruins from the northwest, Lee Gregory, late afternoon, July, 1979.

83: Masonry tower ruins at Hovenweep National Monument, United States Department of the Interior: National Park Service, midday.

85 top: Cliff Palace, State of Colorado: Office of Tourism, midday.

85 bottom: Spruce Tree House, United States Department of the Interior: National Park Service, midday.

91 top: Telluride from the northeast along the Imogene Pass Road, Lee Gregory, morning, September, 1982.

91 bottom: Camp Bird Mine from the west along the Imogene Pass Road, Lee Gregory, afternoon, August, 1981.

95: Bridal Veil Falls from the east end of the Telluride Valley, Lee Gregory, afternoon, July, 1979.

99: Alta boarding house from the southwest, Ken Jessen.

101: Looking northwest from Ophir Pass, Lee Gregory, afternoon, August, 1989.

103: Trout Lake, Colorado Office of Tourism.

105: Lizard Head Peak from the southeast along Colorado 145, Lee Gregory, afternoon, August, 1981.

109: Chimney Rock from the road 0.6 miles west of Owl Creek Pass, Lee Gregory, afternoon, August, 1981.

110: Palisades from the road 6.8 miles east of Owl Creek Pass, Lee Gregory, afternoon, September, 1979.

113: Looking south from Dallas Divide along Colorado 62, Lee Gregory, morning, July, 1982.

115: Box Canyon Falls from inside Box Canyon, Lee Gregory, afternoon, July, 1979.

116: Ouray from the south along US 550, Lee Gregory, afternoon, September, 1979.

119 top: Looking northeast across Engineer Pass from Engineer Mountain, Bureau of Land Management, afternoon.

119 bottom: Looking southeast across the upper Animas Valley from just south of Engineer Mountain, Bureau of Land Management, afternoon.

123: Red Mountain from the northwest along US 550, Lee Gregory, afternoon, September, 1989.

125: Silverton from the south at a turnout along US 550, Lee Gregory, morning, September, 1989.

126: The Durango-Silverton Train, Colorado Office of Tourism.

129: Engineer Mountain from the southeast along US 550, Lee Gregory, morning, September, 1989.

PHOTOGRAPHIC DATA

130: Abrams Mountain from the north at a turnout along US 550 1.5 miles south of Ouray, Lee Gregory, afternoon, September, 1989.

131: Bear Creek Falls from US 550 1.5 miles south of Ouray, Lee Gregory, afternoon, September, 1989.

137: Lake San Cristobal from Colorado 149 5.0 miles south of Lake City, Ken Jessen, afternoon, October, 1983.

139 top: Large building at the eastern edge of Carson, Lee Gregory, morning, August, 1981.

139 bottom: Looking northeast from the Continental Divide toward Carson, Lee Gregory, morning, August, 1981.

140: Looking north from Carson, Lee Gregory, morning, August, 1981.

143: Looking northeast across the Slumgullion Earthflow from the mountainside just west of Lake San Cristobal, Bureau of Land Managment, midday.

145: The San Juan Mountains from the east at Windy Point Overlook, Lee Gregory, morning, September, 1982.

147: North Clear Creek Falls from the overlook, Lee Gregory, morning, September, 1982.

149: Mines on canyon walls just north of Creede, Lee Gregory, midday, August, 1982.

151 top: Looking northwest into Wheeler Geologic Natural Area, Lee Gregory, afternoon, September, 1981.

151 bottom: Looking north into Wheeler Geologic Natural Area, Lee Gregory, afternoon, September, 1981.

157: Del Norte Window from the west, Lee Gregory, afternoon, August, 1979.

159: Looking northwest into the Weminuche Wilderness from Lobo Overlook, Lee Gregory, morning, August, 1982.

161: Looking south from Wolf Creek Pass Overlook, Lee Gregory, morning, September, 1979.

163: Treasure Falls, Lee Gregory, afternoon, August, 1979.

167: Buildings at the northern edge of Summitville from the west along the road, Lee Gregory, afternoon, September, 1981.

171: Lookout Mountain from the southwest along the road, Lee Gregory, afternoon, August, 1989.

175: Cumbres and Toltec train from along Colorado 17, Lee Gregory, afternoon, August, 1989.

181: Great Sand Dunes National Monument from the top of a dune looking toward the Sangre de Cristo Mountains to the north, Bureau of Land Management, early morning.

183: East side of the tunnel through a volcanic dike along the Cordova Pass Scenic Drive 9.6 miles east of Cucharas Pass, Lee Gregory, morning, August, 1982.

PHOTOGRAPHIC DATA

184: The Devil's Staircase from the north along Colorado 12 6.4 miles south of La Veta, Lee Gregory, morning, August, 1982.

187: The south side of Stonewall Gap from the west along Colorado 12, Lee Gregory, afternoon, September, 1978.

189: Looking southeast across Bent's Old Fort, Lee Gregory, afternoon, October, 1981.

Back cover (from left to right):

Marmot from Tincup pass, Bob Schram, midday, July, 1984.

Telluride, from Lizard Head Pass, Nancy White, midday, January, 1978.

Durango-Silverton Narrow Gauge from end of the line, Bob Schram, afternoon, August, 1974.

Large arch in the east rim of Rattlesmake Canyon from the lower level, Lee Gregory, afternoon, May, 1982.

BIBLIOGRAPHY

Athearn, Robert G. *The Denver and Rio Grande Western Railroad*. Lincoln: University of Nebraska Press, 1962.

Baars, Donald L. *The Colorado Plateau: A Geologic History*. Albuquerque: University of New Mexico Press, 1983.

Bancroft, Caroline. *Unique Ghost Towns and Mountain Spots*. Boulder: Johnson Publishing, 1961.

Bartlett, Richard A. *Great Surveys of the American West*. Norman: University of Oklahoma Press, 1962.

Beckner, Raymond M. *Along Colorado Trails*. Canon City, Colo.: Raymond M. Beckner, 1975.

Benham, Jack. *Ouray*. Ouray, Colo.: Bear Creek Publishing, 1976.

Borneman, Walter R., and Lampert, Lyndon J. *A Climbing Guide to Colorado's Fourteeners*. Boulder: Pruett Publishing, 1978.

Bower, Donald E. *Roaming the American West*. New York: Galahad Books, 1971.

Brown, Robert L. *Colorado Ghost Towns: Past and Present*. Caldwell, Id.: Caxton Printers, 1972.

———. *Ghost Towns of the Colorado Rockies*. Caldwell, Id.: Caxton Printers, 1968.

———. *Jeep Trails to Colorado Ghost Towns*. Caldwell, Id.: Caxton Printers, 1963.

Chappell, Gordon, and Hauck, Cornelius W. *Scenic Line of the World*. Golden, Colo.: Colorado Railroad Museum, 1977.

Cheney, Margaret. *Tesla: Man Out of Time*. New York: Dell Publishing, 1981.

Chronic, Halka. *Roadside Geology of Colorado*. Missoula: Mountain Press Publishing, 1980.

Chronic, John, and Chronic, Halka. *Prairie, Peak, and Plateau: A Guide to the Geology of Colorado* (Colorado Geological Survey Bulletin 32). Denver: Colorado Geological Survey, 1972.

Cromie, Alice Hamilton. *Tour Guide to the Old West*. New York: Quadrangle/The New York Times Book Company, 1977.

Dawson, J. Frank. *Place Names in Colorado*. Denver: Golden Bell Press, 1954.

Dolson, John. *The Black Canyon of the Gunnison*. Boulder: Pruett Publishing, 1982.

Eberhart, Perry. *Guide to the Colorado Ghost Towns and Mining Camps*. 4th rev. ed. Chicago: Swallow Press, 1969.

———. *Treasure Tales of the Rockies*. 3d rev. ed. Chicago: Swallow Press, 1969.

Feitz, Leland. *Soapy Smith's Creede*. Colorado Springs: Little London Press, 1973.

Fishbein, Seymour L. (ed.). *Wilderness U.S.A.* Washington, D.C.: National Geographic Society, 1973.

BIBLIOGRAPHY

Folsom, Franklin, and Folsom, Mary Elting. *America's Ancient Treasures*. 3d rev. ed. Albuquerque: Unversity of New Mexico Press, 1983.

Gregory, Lee. *Colorado Scenic Guide: Northern Region*. Boulder: Johnson Publishing, 1983.

Griffiths, Mel, and Rubright, Lynnell. *Colorado: A Geography*. Boulder: Westview Press, 1983.

Grout, William. *Colorado Adventures: Forty Trips in the Rockies*. Denver: Golden Bell Press, 1973.

Hansen, Harry (ed.). *Colorado: A Guide to the Highest State*. Rev. ed. New York: Hastings House, 1970.

Helmers, Dow. *Historic Alpine Tunnel*. Colorado Springs: Century One Press, 1971.

Hilts, Len. *National Forest Guide*. Chicago: Rand McNally, 1978.

Jackson, Earl. *Your National Park System in the Southwest*. 3d rev. ed. Globe, Ariz.: Southwest Parks and Monuments Association, 1976.

Jenkinson, Michael. *Land of Clear Light*. New York: Dutton, 1977.

Kelley, Charles. *The Outlaw Trail: A History of Butch Cassidy and His Wild Bunch*. New York: Bonanza Books, 1959.

Koch, Donald Warner. *The Colorado Pass Book*. Boulder: Pruett Publishing, 1980.

Lavender, David. *David Lavender's Colorado*. Garden City, N.Y.: Doubleday, 1976.

Look, Al. *1,000 Million Years on the Colorado Plateau*. Denver: Golden Bell Press, 1955.

_____. *U-Boom: Uranium on the Colorado Plateau*. Denver: Golden Bell Press, 1956.

Manahan, Patrice (ed.). *Exploring the Unspoiled West: The West Nobody Knows*. Vol. 1. Pasadena, Calif.: Ward Ritchie Press, 1974.

Marshall, Muriel. *Uncompahgre*. Caldwell, Id.: Caxton Printers, 1981.

Matthews, William H., III. *A Guide to the National Parks: Their Landscape and Geology*. Garden City, N.Y.: Doubleday, 1973.

McNitt, Frank. *Richard Wetherill: Anasazi*. Rev. ed. Albuquerque: University of New Mexico Press, 1966.

Oppelt, Norman T. *Guide to Prehistoric Ruins of the Southwest*. Boulder: Pruett Publishing, 1981.

Ormes, Robert M. *Tracking Ghost Railroads in Colorado*. Rev. ed. Colorado Springs: Century One Press, 1980.

Osterwald, Doris B. *Cinders and Smoke: A Mile by Mile Guide for the Durango to Silverton Narrow Gauge Trip*. 2d ed. Lakewood, Colo.: Western Guideways, 1968.

Pearl, Richard M. *Landforms of Colorado*. Colorado Springs: Earth Science Publishing, 1975.

Pike, Donald G. *Anasazi: Ancient People of the Rock*. New York: Crown Publishers, 1974.

BIBLIOGRAPHY

Pixler, Paul. *Hiking Trails of Southwestern Colorado*. Boulder: Pruett Publishing, 1981.

Quirk, Patrick J., and Fise, Thomas F. (eds.). *A Complete Guide to America's National Parks*. Washington, D.C.: National Park Foundation, 1979.

Redford, Robert. *The Outlaw Trail*. New York: Grosset and Dunlap, 1978.

Reed, Allen C. *Grand Circle Adventure*. Las Vegas, Nev.: KC Publications, 1983.

Rigby, J. Keith. *Northern Colorado Plateau*. Dubuque, Iowa: Kendall/Hunt Publishing, 1976.

——. *Southern Colorado Plateau*. Dubuque, Iowa: Kendall/Hunt Publishing, 1977.

Rockwell, Wilson. *Uncompahgre Country*. Denver: Sage Books, 1965.

Roylance, Ward J. *Utah: A Guide to the State*. Part 2, rev. Salt Lake City, Utah: A Guide to the State Foundation, 1982.

Sprague, Marshall. *The Great Gates: The Story of the Rocky Mountain Passes*. Lincoln: University of Nebraska Press, 1964.

State Historical Society of Colorado, The. *Bent's Old Fort*. Denver: The State Historical Society of Colorado, 1979.

Stokes, William Lee; Judson, Sheldon; and Picard, M. Dane. *Introduction to Geology: Physical and Historical*. 2d ed. Englewood Cliffs, N.J.: Prentice-Hall, 1978.

Sumner, David. *Colorado Southwest: The Land . . . the People . . . the History*. Denver: Sanborn Souvenir Company, 1973.

——. *High Rails Over Cumbres: The Story of the Cumbres and Toltec Scenic Railroad*. Denver: Sanborn Souvenir Company, 1976.

Sykes, Jr., George K., and Sumner, David. *Guide to Natural Wonders of the West*. Harrisburg, Penn.: Stackpole Books, 1978.

Trimble, Stephen A. *Great Sand Dunes: The Shape of the Wind*. Globe, Ariz.: Southwest Parks and Monuments Association.

——. *Rim of Time: The Canyons of Colorado National Monument*. Fruita, Colo.: Colorado National Monument Association, 1981.

Ubbelodhe, Carl; Benson, Maxine; and Smith, Duane A. *A Colorado History*. Centennial ed., rev. Boulder: Pruett Publishing, 1976.

Udall, Stewart L. *America's Natural Treasures: National Nature Monuments and Seashores*. Waukesha, Wisc.: Country Beautiful, 1971.

Weber, Rose. *A Quick History of Telluride*. Colorado Springs: Little London Press, 1974.

Wood, Frances Elizabeth, and Wood, Florence Dorothy. *I Hauled These Mountains in Here*. Caldwell, Id.: Caxton Printers, 1977.

Yandell, Michael D. (ed.). *National Parkways: A Photographic and Comprehensive Guide to Rocky Mountain and Mesa Verde National Parks*. Casper, Wyo.: World-Wide Research and Publishing, 1975.

Young, Robert G., and Young, Joann W. *Colorado West: Land of Geology and Wildflowers*. Grand Junction, Colo.: Robert G. Young, 1977.

INFORMATION SOURCES

USDA Forest Service
Rocky Mountain Region
11177 West 8th Avenue
P.O. Box 25127
Lakewood, Colorado 80225

Bureau of Land Management
Colorado State Office
2850 Youngfield Street
Denver, Colorado 80215

National Park Service
United States Department of the Interior
12795 W. Alameda Parkway
P.O. Box 25287
Denver, Colorado 80225

National Cartographic Information Center
United States Geological Survey
Box 25046, Stop 504
Denver Federal Center
Denver, Colorado 80225

Colorado Tourism Board
1625 Broadway, Suite 1700
Denver, Colorado 80202

State of Colorado
Division of Parks and Outdoor Recreation
Room 618
1313 Sherman Street
Denver, Colorado 80203

Durango and Silverton Narrow Gauge Railroad Company
479 Main Avenue
Durango, Colorado 81301
(303) 247-2733

Cumbres and Toltec Scenic Railroad
Post Office Box 668
Antonito, Colorado 81120
(719) 376-5483

INDEX

INDEX

INDEX

INDEX

INDEX TO SITES

STATE MAP

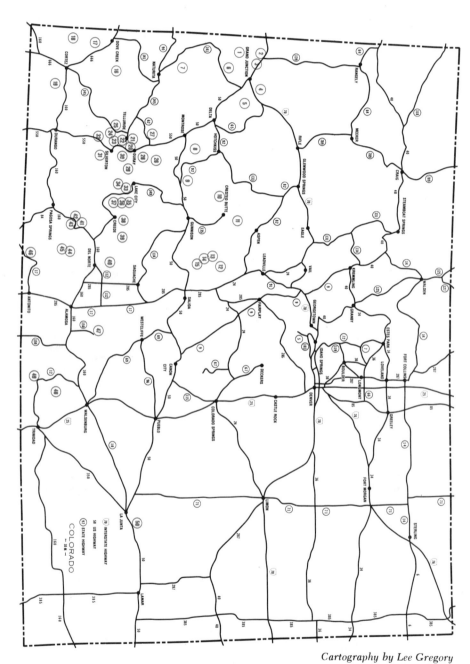

Cartography by Lee Gregory